Beyond RARE

The INFJ's Guide to Cultivating Growth & Self-Awareness

Elaine Schallock Drenth

. CONTENTS .

. ACKNOWLEDGMENTS .

They say it takes a village. In the case of this book, it took two: the storybook Mediterranean seafront town of Vieile Antibes, France–a place I had the great fortune to call home for three months in the course of writing this book–and the tranquil Pacific Ocean retreat, Avila Beach, California, which helped oversee its completion. Both of these waterside havens had direct provenance in this book becoming a reality, confirming yet again that many a precious treasure is birthed by the sea. To the friends and family who graciously welcomed me into their homes there, thank you. I am eternally grateful.

For the enduring works of Carl G. Jung, which have brought and continue to bring clarity and validation to our inner intuitions, the psychic universe and I are incredibly thankful.

To the friends and family who continually encouraged me in this, at times, very challenging process, for providing emotional support and helping me overcome self-doubt along the way, I'm thankful beyond measure.

Last, but in no way least, to my husband, life-partner, mind-mate and best friend, A.J. Drenth, for being the first one to peek under the mantle and see the promise of treasure worth sharing, even when I wasn't convinced there was any value there–thank you my love. It is in no way an exaggeration to say that you're the reason this book exists.

. PREFACE .

The grain of inspiration that set this book into motion began a long time ago, without intentionality–its rudimentary origins a testament to its lack of aspiration at the time. Erupting spontaneously from a desperate need for self-understanding during a time of personal crisis, early excerpts read more like the solipsistic ramblings of an amateur diary keeper than an authority on the subject of personality type. Witness: almost nothing managed to survive its original form in the act of writing this book.

But perhaps I should be more forgiving of these early, feeble attempts at self-understanding since it was from these rough-hewn reflections that a basis for Personality Junkie's INFJ profile was born–the subsequent success of which has earned it the distinction of being the most-viewed personality profile on the website. To date, it remains a high-ranking Google result for INFJ-related searches. As thankful as I am for these achievements, what is most meaningful to me is that these unassuming insights were my salvation at a time when I needed to believe in myself the most.

At the time A.J. Drenth propositioned me to use some of my raw material to overhaul his INFJ type profile, to say I was reluctant would be an understatement. Not only was I hesitant to share the beloved brainchild of my personal experience, I was doubtful that anyone would find perceptible value in the discourse I had penned. Afterall, the blogosphere is already littered with practically anything that a self-proclaimed personality junkie could seek a hit from: type descriptions abound, as do opinions of every sort on everything from careers to relationships. What could I possibly offer to the noise?

Fortunately, A.J. knew his audience better than I did. Indeed, what he had fortuitously discovered early in his blogging days, almost by accident, was the discernable demand from Introverted Intuitives scouring the web for more in-depth analysis on personality type–the sort of material that INFJs are particularly fond of providing–and so, to meet that demand, A.J. boldly took a chance on this rather self-effacing INFJ.

Apropos I think, if not poetic, that an initial act of self-preservation was ultimately transformed into a public offering. In a real way, this book is a continuation of that objective: a dedication to fellow INFJs seeking a deeper understanding of themselves, as well as a practical guide on how to apply that knowledge for a more meaningful life experience. So it is with considerable gratitude for you, dear reader, for desiring to go further in your journey toward self-discovery–to learn about and grow in and through your type–that I share this little bit of treasure with you.

. INTRODUCTION .

Ask any INFJ to recount the tale of his or her path to the realization that he or she is, in fact, an INFJ and you're almost certain to be regaled with the opener: "*Well... I always knew I was different...*" The pervasiveness of this lead-in, matched only by its predictability, has earned INFJs the right to be parodied mercilessly within the personality community–a right gleefully capitalized on by other personality types who understandably resent INFJs laying claim to being different (read: "rare") and the "special" status that rarity implies.

Citing the oft-repeated statistic that INFJs represent the "rarest personality type" of the 16 psychological types (generally thought to be somewhere between 1–3% of the population), INFJs seem to relish informing others of their relative obscurity. Indeed, to hear an INFJ tell it, the seldom experienced "INFJ sighting" is about as probable as chancing upon a yeti playing hopscotch with a group of unicorns flanked by a team of tap-dancing dragons.

To be fair, it's understandable why INFJs, having spent much of their lives with the awareness that they don't exactly fit in with more ubiquitous types, find a degree of comfort–or vindication even–with the discovery that their felt anomalousness is accounted for statistically by way of demographic data on personality type: for many INFJs, this is a first and crucial step toward self-discovery. But while the "rare" distinction can and often does provide a helpful role early in the type identification process (usually when they are trying to make sense of why they feel like such outsiders), too many INFJs simply zero-in on it as their primary basis for self-understanding, embracing the statistic as the core quality that defines their type.

This is problematic on several levels. First, it has already been shown how the "rare" claim understandably invites resentment from other types who perceive INFJs as essentially flaunting their exceptionality as a result of their scarcity among the general population. What is less obvious, however, is how focusing on their rarity is actually something of a red herring, distracting INFJs from the larger goal of individuation and overall personal development. In truth, the problem with being overly consumed with the rarity of one's type has the unfortunate effect of isolating INFJs, not just from others, but from themselves as well.

By encouraging INFJs to rethink the value of clinging to the "rare" distinction, I am hoping readers can acknowledge that, beyond a certain point in development, continuing to hang on to that trophy is little more than an ego ploy that actually undermines INFJs' potential for true personal development. In other words, holding fast to one's "rare" status dissuades meaningful growth by allowing INFJs to rest comfortably on the false assumption that they have "found themselves" by virtue of having discovered their relative scarcity. Moreover, while it's true that INFJs are the least prevalent of the 16 personality types outlined by the Myers-Briggs Type Indicator (MBTI)®, rareness on its own should in no way be equated with being "special" or "exceptional" above others. INFJs inclined to get on their high horse with respect to their rarity might do well to consider that their scarcity could just as easily be interpreted as evidence of their relative *lack* of utility to the overall "psychic economy," as Jung calls it, rather than an indication of their manifest preeminence–not exactly something to get uppity about.

But before I'm accused of betraying my own kind, allow me to enthusiastically affirm that INFJs *do* possess distinct personality traits not readily found among other types; qualities that, if developed properly, are incredibly valuable. However, that development cannot occur if INFJs remain married to the belief that their rarity constitutes the majority of what they have to offer the world. For many INFJ readers, I presume, this suspicion has been brewing in Intuition's pot for a while now. Indeed, the very nature of Introverted Intuition (Ni) is that it's not long satisfied with one level of knowing before demanding to go further. I have to believe that more than a few INFJs have reached a point of critical dissatisfaction with the constant drum-banging about their rarity and have grown hungry for something more meaningful to sink their proverbial teeth into.

It's that inner impetus that I'm appealing to here. Directly, INFJs ready to move toward growth and actualization must be prepared to conceive of their identity as something that exists independent of the "rarity" claim and the apparent prestige that goes along with that distinction; to make a shift in self-conceit, grammatically and paradigmatically, from the merely descriptive to the prescriptive–in other words, from *being* "beyond rare" to *going* "beyond rare."

• • •

In advising readers to go "beyond rare," I am, of course, referring to the specific term, however–and perhaps more importantly–I am referring to seeing the value that exists in a personality nomenclature that goes beyond the merely descriptive. That's because there is tremendous wisdom to be gleaned when we move past a preliminary understanding of personality types as a laundry list of static traits or terms (e.g., type profiles) toward an application-based approach to self-growth.

In saying this, it is not my intention to disparage the value of type descriptions; indeed, for many people, this is often a necessary starting point for personality newcomers, as scouring type profiles often brings a great deal of initial awareness, interest and enjoyment to the field of personality psychology. But for the vast majority of those who have familiarized themselves with the descriptions afforded by Jung's *Psychological Types* or the MBTI®, this is essentially where the journey ends–before it ever really begins.

Personality enthusiasts wishing to go deeper may be surprised to discover how much more typology has to offer than first meets the eye by way of mere type descriptions. In truth, personality type is not static, as these descriptions might suggest, but incredibly dynamic. It has been my experience that those who denounce the validity of personality theory often do so as a knee-jerk response to the suggestion that they are being boxed-in by a fixed set of one-sided traits. However understandable, this reaction represents a failure to grasp the complexity of Jungian psychological theory (of which personality type is merely a part), as much or more than a failure of personality theory itself.

In reality, the personality equation actually reads more like a map than a laundry list, serving an important role in the more complex psychological process Jung calls *individuation*–a concept I alluded to earlier. So what is "individuation" exactly? Jung defines it thusly:

> *Individuation is an expression of that biological process–as simple or complicated as the case may be–by which every living thing becomes what it was destined to become from the beginning.* [1]

More specifically, it's the act of integrating in consciousness previously unconscious parts of ourselves in order to achieve wholeness, or the realization of what Jung calls the "self" (the entire personality). Put simply, it's the process by which you become You, with a capital "Y."

Individuation is the ultimate aim, conscious or not, of all living things. And it's inextricably linked to personality psychology insofar as personality type provides the blueprint for the specific parts of ourselves that have already been differentiated in consciousness (the "found" parts), along with those that remain unrealized in the unconscious (the "lost" parts). Unwittingly, we become players in a drama that sees us striving to reclaim the "lost" parts of our personality—often contrary to what we know to be our "authentic" selves—in an attempt to spur the individuation process.

Of course, these various parts of our personality—the conscious and unconscious, the differentiated and undifferentiated, the lost and found—vary based on our type and stage of development. It is our task to discover which particular parts we have in play, and then work to realize them with maximum effectiveness in order to define ourselves as unique individuals. Jung elegantly captures that charge in the following way:

> *Personality is the supreme realization of the innate idiosyncrasy of a living being. It is an act of high courage flung in the face of life, the absolute affirmation of all that constitutes the individual, the most successful adaptation to the universal conditions of existence coupled with the greatest possible freedom of self-determination.*[2]

For this reason, we cannot discount the value of personality type within the larger context of self-growth and individuation.

A moment ago, I referred to personality type being like a map as opposed to a laundry list. However, it may be more accurate to view the individuation process itself as the map or journey, with one's personality type being more like the *key* or *legend*, its terms specific to the individual using it. Familiarizing ourselves with the various terms is absolutely essential since, without them, it would be difficult, if not impossible, to decipher the map; but that's precisely the point—the terms are *meant to be utilized* toward a larger end.

Beginning and ending the type discovery process with the basic descriptions and terminology is tantamount to reading the key but then failing to apply that information to the map itself. Entertaining? Sure. Enlightening? Not terribly. And never is this more problematic than when we hone in on parts of the descriptions that highlight our more favorable or illustrious qualities while turning a blind eye to the more *ahem* *objectionable* ones. Too often, we simply fixate on aspects of the type descriptions that we like best because they make us feel good about ourselves; such is arguably true for INFJs who continue their unyielding allegiance to the "rare" distinction as central to their self-concept.

It bears reminding that rarity itself is *not* a recognized trait in the Jungian personality taxonomy. Moreover, mere awareness of one's relative scarcity provides little to no guidance for how to go about growing, or individuating, psychospiritually. In reality, true rarity is the individual of *any* type who is able to successfully individuate through mastery of the entire function stack–an achievement that is only made possible by relinquishing the ego attachments that keep us from honestly assessing all elements (favorable or not) that constitute our personality type and whole self.

This constitutes no small act of bravery. Such a move requires INFJs to open themselves to other relevant parts of their personality that go beyond their rarity. And while this includes more luminous facets of the INFJ type, such as Intuition and Feeling, it also entails the weaker qualities stored up in Sensing and Thinking that INFJs tend to repress. INFJs seeking self-growth must therefore be willing to not only embrace their strengths, but also confront their inner demons since, at the risk of sounding cliché, it's only through the desert that we ever reach the Promised Land.

INFJs up to the task will hopefully find within this book the necessary tools to guide them along that journey in the form of compassionate, if occasionally uncomfortable, insight. My hope is that readers experience this book as a sort of journey in itself; one that may be referenced again and again whenever life brings spiritual and psychological challenges, as it inevitably does from time to time.

• • •

Meaningful growth demands that we endure some measure of discomfort; it's unavoidable. In asking my fellow INFJs to dispense with the rarity rubric, I am, in effect, asking INFJs everywhere to slacken their grip on the ego defenses keeping the oyster mantle closed. The truth is this: INFJs attempting to protect their valuables by keeping the shell clamped shut are conflating *potential* treasure (the flesh) with *realized* treasure (the pearl); and being unwilling to let some grit under the mantle—an understandable however misguided attempt at self-preservation—robs INFJs of the opportunity to transform the storehouse of potential value they possess into true and lasting wealth.

That's where this book comes in. Its contents are an attempt to spur the transformation process that ultimately sees INFJs turning their incredible potential into value-realized, both personally and in the world around them: my pearl, your grit. I realize the task sounds daunting. I have, however, done my best to polish off the rough edges in an effort to make the experience more inviting. I'm hopeful readers will find the reward worth the effort; and it beats the alternative, anyway: being shucked around with involuntarily. INFJs wishing to avoid the pain of being forcibly pried open and mercilessly prodded, I think, will prefer the former.

Finally, I'm obligated to make one additional disclaimer. In case it wasn't evident up to this point, this book cannot fairly be described as an "Intro to INFJs." It really reads more like an intermediate or even advanced-level book on personality type. The material presented here presumes that readers are at least minimally conversant with the terms and theories outlined by Jung and Myers-Briggs. Readers should not only be familiar with the eight preferences (Introversion, Extraversion, Intuition, Sensing, Thinking, Feeling, Judging, Perceiving), but also the eight functions (Ni, Ne, Si, Se, Ti, Te, Fi, Fe) and "function stack" (particularly that of the INFJ.)

While I have included a glossary with these and other relevant terms, it's really intended as a convenience only in the course of reading this book. Readers who are not fully comfortable with the aforementioned concepts are advised to review them on the Personality Junkie website prior to undertaking this book. Other recommended introductory reads include A.J. Drenth's *The 16*

Personality Types, Lenore Thomson's *Personality Type: An Owner's Manual,* and Carl Jung's *Psychological Types* (the original authority on the psychological types, and my personal favorite).

With the above in mind, this book is divided into sections, like a trilogy, with each section containing three chapters apiece. Section I familiarizes readers with the more well-known known traits of INFJs, bringing further understanding to the processes of Intuition, Introversion, and Feeling. INFJs should find welcome camaraderie in Chapters 1–3, particularly if they are struggling with feeling misunderstood, as much of what is presented will likely validate facets of the INFJ with which they're already aware, just on a deeper level.

Section II, comprising Chapters 4–6, encourages INFJs to come to terms with the less well-known traits buried in the lower half of the function stack. It primarily examines the murky realms of INFJs' unconscious side and is dedicated to understanding how they approach matters pertaining to the Sensing realm, e.g., security, physicality, and the problem of moving into action. It also confronts the thorny problem of perfectionism that notoriously plagues INFJs, giving context to its origins. An awareness of these often underdeveloped traits is essential to bring significance to the INFJ's individuation process, which naturally leads to...

...Section III–what I consider the most critical material presented with respect to personal growth. Chapters 7–9 dive headlong into the individuation process itself and deal with the tribulations that often arise from INFJs' struggle to reconcile and integrate the personality elements described in Sections I and II. It includes an intimate look at INFJs at their most vulnerable, as well as how to confront the personal demons necessary to overcome self-doubt in order to find peace, self-acceptance, and eventually actualize their full potential.

So now, bold reader, with the necessary caveats and introductions behind us, let's take a swim...

1. SELF-DISCOVERY (n.)

"He who would search for pearls must dive below..."

John Dryden

It's a curious thing to contemplate how human beings ever evolved to feel compelled to embark on this process we call "self-discovery": the act of understanding our inner nature, of knowing who and what we are on the deepest level possible. Presumably, the impetus has existed ever since the conscious mind first realized its potential for self-reflexivity–a prerequisite for self-discovery. Of course, at what point the mind evolved to become self-reflexive is yet another question without an answer. But despite these and other life riddles, what is perhaps most curious is the varied and unique ways we each go about the process of self-discovery.

For Sensing types, especially those of the Extraverted variety, knowing "who they are" is generally something that can only be revealed in the course of actively living one's life (the expression, "*Figuring it out as I go...*" was surely coined by an Extraverted Sensor). This is in no way a knock on Extraverted Sensing (ES) types–they're simply taking one of many viable paths toward self-understanding. The advantage of this approach is it allows them to experience a great many things without having to worry about the hows and whys that might otherwise limit the scope of what they might accomplish in the relatively short span of a lifetime.

Another way of understanding the self-discovery process for ES types is as something generally revealed to them after the fact, or *a posteriori*. This means knowing what they value and who they are cannot be deduced in advance of actually experiencing life and gathering concrete information from the world around them. Afterall, how can one know what options or experiences resonate without actually trying them first? From their perspective, attempting to "find oneself"—a turn of phrase they relish rolling eyes at—is largely regarded as a fool's errand, apt to be as fruitful as tracking down Bigfoot.

The implication here is that self-discovery contains two key elements not prominently featured in Extraverted and Sensing types: namely, the "self" element and the "discovery" element. Self-discovery is concerned with (a) what specifically distinguishes us as individuals (the "self," or Introverted element) and (b) what our primary purpose is (the "discovery," or Intuition, element). This suggests that the process of self-discovery is largely an Introverted and Intuitive one which tends to beckon IN types in particular.

Now, before leaping up in protest with counterexamples (I hear you, clever Intuitive!), allow me to acknowledge that things get murkier when we talk about Introverted Sensing (IS) and Extraverted Intuitive (EN) types. Without wading too deeply into the specifics of type, Introverted Sensors are more likely to tackle the "self" element—knowing what distinguishes them as individuals, often with respect to their physical likes and dislikes—but without belaboring the hows and whys of what got them there. Extraverted Intuitives, by contrast, are more likely to relish the "discovery" element, enthusiastically grappling with questions of purpose and meaning, but they often struggle to implement those philosophies in a way that specifically defines who they are as individuals or clearly articulates their particular life path.

Quibbles over type overlaps aside, the fact remains that self-discovery (at least as it relates to self-understanding) is usually of paramount importance to IN types, especially earlier in life than is generally true for ES types. Their life path demands that self-discovery precede action–in other words, it's *a priori.* With Introversion dominating the directional focus inward and Intuition orchestrating the conceptual information gathering, IN types feel they must know themselves, including their higher purpose, before knowing what "to do" with their lives. So begins the arduous task of endeavoring to "know thyself" in order to "be thyself" for IN types.

• • •

Quintessential "late-bloomers," Introverted Intuitives may postpone major life decisions regarding career, marriage, and children (decisions that Extraverted Sensors tend to undertake earlier in life) in favor of activities aimed at self-exploration. This charge comes rather easily to young Introverted Intuitives who engage in self-exploration instinctively, if rather unconsciously. Even as children, they are weighing their experiences in the outside world against their inner conceptual impressions. They learn to seek solitude and turn inward where they can process their thoughts, feelings, and intuitions without outside interference. It's through these early practices that IN types begin forging small trails of self-exploration which ultimately clear the path for self-discovery.

While this holds true for IN types generally, at some point during the development process, the path of self-exploration bifurcates for Introverted Intuitive Perceivers (INPs) and Introverted Intuitive Judgers (INJs). INPs start the explorative process by using internally established frameworks of either Introverted Feeling (Fi) or Introverted Thinking (Ti) to help guide them in their search for external conceptions or philosophies (Ne) that resonate with these inner feelings (Fi) or logic (Ti). Like astronauts and explorers, INPs chase the stars and wind of collective consciousness in an attempt to funnel as many theories as possible through an internal sifting process that eventually sees them constructing a definitive worldview and, with it, their unique place in the universe.

But what about INJs—what does the self-exploration process look like for them? Setting aside the controversial nature of the "different / rare" distinction, there may actually be something worth gleaning in the first three words of the statement, "*I always knew I was different*": a telling allusion to the use of Introverted Intuition (Ni) leading the self-discovery process. This "always knowing" is a defining feature of Introverted Intuition (Ni)—the function exhibited most prominently in INJ types. When INJs endeavor to "know themselves," they begin the search inwardly, drawing from their internal well of knowledge for insight that they then attempt to organize, or make sense of, vis-à-vis externally established frameworks.

Such is the nature of Introverted Intuition: an ever-flowing fount of subconscious knowledge that reveals itself metaphorically via the language of symbolic imagery. Even at an early age, INJs are compelled to seek Intuition's counsel for practically everything, slowly establishing a pattern of trust between the INJ "apprentice" and her Ni "advisor." Wherever a situation demands insight or clarity, the INJ is poised, bucket in hand, to retrieve wisdom from Ni's well. This intimate communion with Ni typically marks the first foray into the realm of self-discovery for INJs.

The above suggests that the self-discovery process for INJs is not so much one of actively identifying and assembling, piece-by-piece, the subjective preferences of Thinking or Feeling, as it is for INPs, but rather one of "passive exhumation" in which the self is more an eternal entity waiting to be discovered, dusted-off, and dissected. In other words, from the perspective of INJs, the self is neither derived from nor dictated by concepts from without, but pre-existent and therefore intuitively "known" all along, regardless of whether it has a name or definition.

In a way, one could make the argument that, for INJs, the quest for self-discovery has relatively little to do with the "self" at all, at least where the self is narrowly construed as an internal adjudicator of personal likes and dislikes. That's because, when INJs talk about "knowing themselves," what they're really referring to is knowing their inner *intuitions*, not their subjective emotional or practical preferences (i.e., what we might normally associate with self-discovery.) However, even this is somewhat misleading since INJs may not feel comfortable claiming their intuitions as "theirs" per se, instead viewing them more as the property or universal domain of prevailing wisdom– available to anyone willing and able to seek them out.

Yet, insofar as INJs recognize that tapping Introverted Intuition is an essential part of who they are, the argument can be made that their self-discovery process is just as legitimate as that of INPs, however different. The main difference lies in the fact that self-discovery for INJs occurs more passively, in a way, by first attempting to understand the essential nature of the self as something more broadly conceived (i.e., "What makes anyone *anyone*?") before zeroing in on traits specific to them as individuals (i.e., "What makes me *me*?").

By drawing on observations from Extraverted Sensing (their inferior function) and material arising from the collective unconscious, INJ types start catching on to the patterns reflected in the objects, people and experiences around them–the early work of Ni. Eventually, these patterns find themselves mirrored in a framework of some sort. In the event that such a framework does not yet exist (a distinct possibility), INJs will draw on their Judging functions to articulate their intuitions via linguistic (Fe) or logical (Te) proofs. Early on, however, Ni is more apt to establish validity by seeking reflection in pre-existing external frameworks rather than by manufacturing its own. Once again, the path of self-exploration sees a fork in the road, this time dividing INTJs and INFJs.

• • •

For INTJs, Introverted Intuitions will most likely be reflected scientifically, in the systems resonant with Extraverted Thinking. Typically, this leads INTJs toward the "physical" sciences where the focus is primarily on laws governing the behavior of objects in fields such as physics, mathematics, and chemistry, rather than those that oversee human behavior. The handful of INTJs that do pursue fields like psychology are more apt to zero in on areas like childhood trauma, cognitive dysfunction, or abnormal psychology which tend to focus on individual aberrations in the collective system or environment–something that appeals to their Te and Fi functions. As a rule, however, most INTJs would rather deal with systems than people.

INFJs, by contrast, are primarily drawn to the humanities, where many of Introverted Intuition's abstract observations regarding truths governing human behavior are reflected in fields like literature, theology, psychology and philosophy. With Extraverted Feeling's emphasis on the collective or "shared" aspects of the human condition, INFJs usually favor frameworks that broadly depict standard deviations within the neurotypical population, rather than looking at individual outliers or abnormalities. Many of INFJs' observations about human nature are echoed in works of fiction, such as books and movies, where character studies play a central role. For this reason, many INFJs are avid students of film and literature.

For the most part, these truths regarding human behavior are merely "implied" so long as they remain in the domain of fiction. Only by moving away from the arts and humanities into more "scientific" fields does Ni get the luxury of having explicit explanations of its hunches revealed. It's here, in fields like psychology, that abstract concepts are finally given definite names and terms. It might be said that if INTJs are your typical fans of science fiction, INFJs would be devotees of *fiction science* if such a genre existed; instead of drawing on scientific fact to speculate on the implications for human behavior, it would rely on observations of human behavior to establish scientific facts or principles.

INFJs attempting to explicate the innate differences of character among psychologically healthy individuals (truths which Ni has likely "known" but struggled to articulate) often experience an "*aha!*" moment with the discovery of personality psychology and related fields of study; finally the formless content of Ni is given something concrete to hang its metaphorical hat on. With the proper vocabulary in hand, INFJs can get to work organizing people by their predominant traits and behaviors, utilizing the proper terms and definitions that help them make sense of the variances in character and temperament which have long been observed but never clearly formulated.

From this point, it's usually not long before INFJs turn the search inward, making the connective leap from the personality traits they observe in others to their *own* personality type. Not surprisingly, the preference INFJs tend to recognize in themselves almost immediately is Intuition, specifically Ni, as the dominant function. Afterall, it's the strength of Ni that likely led them to sense that they were "different" in the first place. That this trait has a name is typically a welcomed relief to INFJs who feel vindicated in having "intuited their own Intuition," so to speak. By fulfilling its own prophesy in a way, Ni earns pride of place in INFJs' core self-concept.

• • •

In order to comprehensively conduct a discussion of INFJs' process of self-discovery, it's necessary at this point to expound on something that's been implied but not expressly stated: INFJs' core sense of self is practically *synonymous* with their psychological type.

Ruminate on that for just a moment.

The INFJ's core sense of self is practically synonymous with his or her psychological type. This is a profound assertion, but, to my knowledge, rarely discussed in typology circles despite being a pivotal point of realization for INFJs. It's also a useful point–if readers will forgive the detour–at which to readily weed out INFPs operating under the false assumption that they are INFJs. That's because such an assertion is almost guaranteed to elicit a negative, knee-jerk response from INFPs' dominant function, Fi, which typically resists the idea of "reducing" an individual's unique and varied facets to a single type label. Presuming to tell an INFP who she is as a person (or anyone else for that matter) on the basis of ready-made categories tends to fly in the face of Fi's unyielding conviction that the thing itself (i.e., the individual) is the only agent with the authority to define itself.

On closer examination, at the heart of this difference of opinion is another question: to what extent is the self something we create versus something that is predetermined from birth? While I wager that the most objective answer to this question is a combination of both, for our purposes the "objective" answer doesn't matter all that much. Ultimately what matters here is what we *subjectively perceive* to be true since this points to key personality differences between INFPs and INFJs. INFPs are more apt to resonate with the idea that the core self is "created" or the product of conditioning, while INFJs are more likely to see it as something more innate or predetermined.

From the INFP's perspective, external personality assessments may be informative, but they don't dictate one's core self-concept–only the INFP has the authority to do that. Consistent with this viewpoint is INFPs' belief that only the individual can determine his or her "best fit" type–in other words, type is primarily a designation of *their choosing*, not something chosen *for them* by nature. For these reasons, an INFP is no more likely to surrender to character evaluations imposed on them by others than an INTP is to the logic of externally sanctioned rules and regulations.

For these reasons, it's not surprising that relying on personality type as the primary basis for understanding an individual naturally leaves a bitter taste in INFPs' mouth. I advise readers experiencing such a reaction to take a moment to honestly consider whether this rings true for them and, if it does, to open themselves to the possibility that they may, in fact, be INFPs. It behooves no one–*especially* INFPs–to labor through the process of individuation under the false assumption that they're INFJs; far better to pause your efforts here and do some deeper research on your true type (see, coincidentally, A.J. Drenth's *My True Type*) before needlessly advancing through this book.

True INFJs, however, will likely resonate with the concept that their psychological type and core self are largely synonymous. The reason for this, the theory goes, is that the dominant function (and, to a lesser degree, the other functions) shapes our perception of what we value most, both in ourselves and in the world around us. Insofar as what we value forms the basis for who we believe ourselves to be as individuals, our psychological type–and, in particular, the dominant function–has direct provenance in how we conceive our core self.

Put another way, we might say, "I *am* what my personality type *values*"– realizing, of course, that relatively few people make the conscious connective leap to typology as a determinant of those individual values, they only know that they do, in fact, possess them. For example, ask an INTP to describe how he sees himself and he'll likely respond with something like, "I'm a rational, independent thinker who enjoys working autonomously (Ti) to explore various intellectual and philosophical pursuits (Ne)." That response gives a direct nod to the presence of dominant Ti and auxiliary Ne in the function stack. He may never state outright that he identifies as an INTP, but he has nevertheless alluded to that reality in his response.

The same concept holds true for INFPs who are apt to express who they are in the following way: "I'm a compassionate individual whose unique upbringing and life experiences have led me to be passionate about 'X' (insert personal passion on behalf of Fi here), and I enjoy exploring creative ways (Ne) of expressing that passion." Though INFPs' specific life experiences, personal values, and methods for implementation will vary, the underlying formula, which is typology based, is nevertheless consistent. In other words, no matter how the particulars differ, all INFPs tend to prioritize their personal Fi values (whatever they may be) above other qualities.

To summarize, if we define our core self by what we value most about ourselves, and if what we value most about ourselves is firmly rooted in the dominant function, then it could be said that our core self is, in many ways, synonymous with our type. But here's the distinctly revelatory coup for INFJs: if what INFJs value most about themselves is whatever best-fit theory Ni has exhumed and refined over the course of its life with respect to human behavior, and if the theory of psychological types *is* that best-fit theory, it logically follows that type theory–in particular the INFJ's own type–and the INFJ's core self are essentially one and the same. Radically conceived, we might say the INFJ is type theory manifested–*idée incarnée.* It would certainly explain why INFJs tend to be the fiercest protectors of type theory since the defense of type theory is, in a very real way, a defense of the self for INFJs.

• • •

As previously illustrated, it is, quite simply, impossible to understand the process of self-discovery for INFJs absent an in-depth discussion of Ni. INFJs hoping to better understand themselves with the aim of moving toward self-actualization should embrace the opportunity to put the workings of Ni under the microscope. However, doing so requires INFJs to risk dispelling the myth that they are somehow more elusive and mystifying than they really are–a narrative that has historically gone hand-in-hand with the "rare" claim.

Again, INFJs who are unwilling to reveal their trade secrets all the while touting their rarity find themselves at cross-purposes with the higher Self. Attempting to protect Ni by making Wizard of Oz style claims to "pay no attention to the man behind the curtain!" sabotages INFJs' efforts by alienating those who might benefit from their insights. In truth, the INFJ's calling in life is not to encourage confusion or obscurity by claiming that they alone have insight into things no one else can understand, but to cast light on that which has been previously shrouded in darkness. That charge is wonderfully captured in a quote from *The Glass Menagerie* by Tennessee Williams:

> *Yes, I have tricks in my pocket. I have things up my sleeve. But I am the opposite of a stage magician. He gives you illusion that has the appearance of truth. I give you truth in the pleasant disguise of illusion.*[3]

It's easy to see why INFJs have developed a reputation for being mysterious and enigmatic (to this day Jung himself continues to be labeled a "mystic," even by Intuitive types who should know better): for a large segment of the population, Intuitives seem to be speaking an entirely different language. But although their ideas may in many respects be different from others, they needn't necessarily be viewed as ineffable or incomprehensible. It may be because INFJs themselves don't really understand *how* Introverted Intuition works (they just know that it somehow works for them) that the Ni process remains shrouded in mystery. This is complicated by the fact that understanding the inner nature of Ni paradoxically *requires* Ni, forcing INFJs to riddle themselves this: Is Ni really the best objective judge of itself?... And thus the reputation of Ni being a mystery contained within a puzzle wrapped in yet another enigma endures.

• • •

Assuming that Ni is somehow capable of de-mystifying itself, especially where it has the ability to more objectively observe Ni at work in others, a closer look at its essential nature is warranted. However, in order to grasp the nature of Ni, it helps to understand Intuition generally. Both Intuition and its opposite, Sensing, are what are known as "perceiving" preferences, so-named because they perceive, or *take in* information, as opposed to organizing it the way the "judging" preferences (Thinking and Feeling) do. Regarding Intuition specifically, Jung associates it with the unconscious due to its involvement with the abstract concepts behind perceptible Sensing phenomena. I would argue that the term "unconscious" is somewhat misleading however as it implies that we cannot really know the contents of Intuition in consciousness. In truth, the "unconscious" material brought up by Intuition is in many ways *more conscious* to Intuitive types than the Sensing world itself.

To understand this better, it helps to conceive Sensing and Intuition as two sides of the same coin: the one cannot escape its relationship with the other. Contained in every explicit object (S) is an implicit concept (N), and vice-versa. That's the nature of Sensing and Intuition. The explicit and the implicit. The thing and the idea. The material and the conceptual. The concrete and the abstract. The actual and the possible. As an aside, these sorts of dichotomies are what form the basis of much of Jung's work on personality type and on psychological development generally.

For Intuitives, perceiving implied concepts comes more naturally than observing and experiencing the world through the five senses alone. What we call "knowing" is entirely possible for Intuitive types without the benefit of direct experience. An Intuitive type, especially with the aid of conceptual frameworks and formulae, can calculate the movement of an object of a certain mass and velocity and "know" its trajectory, without having to physically test it. Yet for Sensing types, this type of "knowledge" without experience seems too abstract and hypothetical, and therefore more difficult to accept absent the kind of "hands-on" proof they prefer to rely on.

There are plenty of things about which Sensors and Intuitives can agree when it comes to easily observable phenomena, but things have a habit of taking a testy turn whenever Intuitives attempt to move beyond the immediate empirical realm and begin extrapolating theories from theories instead. The more leaps of inference–or degrees of conceptual separation–between an observable phenomenon and a working theory ("*if this then that, and if that then this...*" thinking), the harder it is for Sensing types to follow Intuitives down the rabbit hole of abstract knowledge.

It's difficult enough to find agreement when Intuitives present a concept to Sensors that has no connection whatsoever to the observable universe (ever heard of black holes?), but the fallout can be catastrophic–Copernican, even–if ever they present an idea or theory that appears to violate basic sense perceptions (e.g. the earth moving around the sun rather than vice-versa). It's against the headwinds of such skepticism that Intuitive types forge on, following Intuition's lead because it knows no other way of knowing. Intuition has taught them that seeing isn't always believing and that our senses can, and often do, play tricks on our powers of perception.

Therefore, when Jung associates Intuition with the "unconscious," in a way he's right, as much of what Intuition perceives has not yet been broadly registered in collective consciousness. However, given sufficient time and research (along with the conversion of enough believers–a biggie) a theory may eventually gain admission into public consciousness. It is with this aim of bringing the "unconscious" content of what *theoretically is* (in the case of Ni) or what *potentially could be* (Ne) into external consciousness that Intuitives carry on in their search for the as yet unknown.

For Extraverted Intuitives (i.e., Ne types), the search for knowledge typically leads them to sniff out ideational potential that is inspired by prior experience, always asking, "but what if *this* were possible?..." True creatives and inventors, Ne types love imagining what doesn't exist currently, but possibly *could* given the right conceptual blueprint. Inspired by the wisdom of enduring experience, they often use this as a launchpoint for imagining conceptual possibilities (e.g. "*Look at how birds fly. What if we could make people fly? How could we do that?...*").

Jung describes Extraverted Intuitives as possessing a strength of "outlook." In a similar vein, I describe them as theory "infusers." Consistent with the Extraverted attitude of Ne, they are consistently looking to add, or *infuse*, more ideas, more theoretical possibilities into the collective Intuitive pot. Sure, some might be duds, but throw enough darts, the theory goes, and eventually you'll land a bulls-eye. Extraverted Intuitives find their stride by rapidly darting across vast conceptual waters to cover as much theoretical sea as possible. From their perspective, netting as many theories as they can gives the best chance of arriving at truth; it's simply antithetical to Ne types to put all their Intuitive eggs into one theoretical basket. Diversification is the pathway to their success, Intuition wise, and for this reason, many fancy themselves polymaths more than experts in any one specific field.

Contrast this with the Introverted attitude of Intuition found in Ni types. Deep-sea divers and cave spelunkers by nature, Introverted Intuitives prefer to go deep where Extraverted Intuitives go broad in the quest for knowledge. Theirs is a different type of treasure hunt: Ni types prefer to go all-in by hunting down one priceless jewel rather than many small baubles. Ni knows that the most valuable gems can only be found through bypassing the more obvious, exposed landscapes that the Ne multitude has already swept. This is what ultimately compels Introverted Intuitives to broach the deep, dark corners of the Intuitive universe that Extraverted Intuitives are generally too impatient to tarry in.

As a rule, Ni types tend to be less enamored with hypothetical possibilities that are largely the future's domain (Jung's "outlook" for Ne types), instead preferring to understand the profundity behind what already exists (Jung's "insight" for Ni types). In other words, where Ne looks ahead of what currently is, Ni tends to look behind, or into, it. In contrast with Ne's penchant for idea "infusion," the Ni process is one of "extraction"–the act of carefully distilling the most refined theoretical essence from the informational swamp. Indeed, Introverted Intuitives can be something of theoretical purists. From Ni's perspective, there is always one best-fit theory. Even if it consists of a complicated series of working parts, a common conceptual thread always exists.

Readers may recognize romanticized versions of Ni at work which have been represented many times over in the form of detective folklore fiction with characters such as Sherlock Holmes whose powers of deduction, particularly on film, are often portrayed as a sudden flash of insight (Ni) that arises concurrently with a slideshow of seemingly insignificant, disparate visual images relayed in rapid succession (Se). Naturally, the more confounding the Se images or evidence, the more brilliant the Ni insight appears to be. This is how, out of many possible theories for what could have happened, Ni manages to suss out the one theory that best explains what actually did, at least in the eyes of these writers and filmmakers.

What I find particularly amusing about these portrayals is how often it's implied that our Ni detective has "consciously" picked up on sensory details completely overlooked by others (i.e. Sensing types)–a technique designed to enhance the mystique surrounding Ni types. In reality, however, Ni rarely recalls sensory details with the sort of razor-sharp precision depicted in these fictional tropes. By far, what is more within Ni's conscious grasp is the intuitive *impression* that arises from the onslaught of sensory data being presented, most of which is actually absorbed unconsciously.

All of this is a roundabout way of saying that the INJ type's dominant function (Ni) is their *most* conscious psychological process, while their inferior function (Se) is the least conscious–a key principle of type theory. But here is where the myth of Ni mystification begins to unravel: contrary to appearances, the insights of Ni aren't actually being pulled out of thin air (though it can certainly *seem* that way, both to observers and even to INJs at times). In truth, Ni derives its insights from concrete data which is actively absorbed by and stored in the Se unconscious (the so-called "thin air"). If depth psychology has taught us anything, it's that the unconscious mind is always at work; and so it is that an abundance of Sensory data is unwittingly uploaded into the INJ's unconscious until, like the classic game of telephone, it finds egress in consciousness, but in an entirely different language: that of Introverted Intuition.

The process by which information is somehow transmitted from the largely unconscious realm of Se up to Ni where the INJ can consciously access it, often remains something of a mystery—at least until the INJ can retrace his steps and solve the puzzle resulting in demystification. Albert Einstein, without directly linking it to typology, alludes to this process, saying:

> *A new idea comes suddenly and in a rather intuitive way. That means it is not reached by conscious logical conclusions. But, thinking it through afterwards, you can always discover the reasons which have led you unconsciously to your guess and you will find a logical way to justify it. Intuition is nothing but the outcome of earlier intellectual experience.*[4]

I would modify Einstein's last sentence, however, by replacing the word "intellectual" with "psychological," which allows for the inclusion of sensory experience as a part of the process that gives rise to the intuition.

One final point I wish to highlight from our example of Ni sleuthery pertains to the relative paleness in empirical (Se) observational skills of the general public vis-à-vis those of the Holmesian hero, which reveals a larger and more powerful psychological truth: namely, the suggestion that the mind is capable of performing certain tasks unconsciously on our behalf better than we can do consciously. This is the first lesson in the power of the unconscious and a fact about which INFJs are likely already familiar. Indeed, it's on this very concept that INFJs have pretty much staked their claim, ideologically, and life's purpose: the belief that the vast majority of human potential remains buried under a sea of conscious knowledge and, to get to it, we have to be willing to go beyond what we think we know about the world and, perhaps more importantly, *ourselves.*

• • •

INFJs—with their powers of insight into the obscurer aspects of the psyche—are in a unique position to light the way for humankind down the dark and shadowy corridor of the unconscious. For those who succeed in this charge, the reward is essentially psychospiritual enlightenment. But this is a monumental task in more ways than one: it means INFJs not only have to convince people that something actually exists under the surface of conscious knowledge, but assuming this is even possible, that proceeding to venture into the darkness is an act worth pursuing at all. As a rule, it's not uncommon for INFJs to find a paucity of takers.

Moreover, because it's impossible to cast light on the shadows of the collective unconscious without also illuminating the personal unconscious, INFJs must be willing to lead by example, which means partaking of the same bitter fare they're dishing out to others. Again, it's not unusual for INFJs to find they're the only ones at the table. In truth, because INFJs' Intuitive process is an Introverted one, they are often forced to take their first fathoms into the waters of the unconscious alone anyway. Fittingly perhaps, it's only in the stillness of solitude that the outside world fades away enough such that INFJs can sink below the surface of conscious experience and follow the current of rich imagery flowing from the subaqueous abyss downward, back to its origins on the seafloor of eternal unconscious knowledge.

2. INTROVERSION (n.)

"Secret, and self-contained, and solitary as an oyster."

Charles Dickens

One evening my girlfriends and I were enjoying dinner at our favorite local Mexican restaurant when the conversation turned to the topic of personality type. Self-admitted novices in the area of personality psychology, they were asking me to explain some of the key personality traits that distinguish us from one another. I enthusiastically obliged, mostly covering the basics of Extraversion and Introversion (usually a good starting place) by explaining our respective types and then elaborating with examples and anecdotes.

This little lesson lasted nearly an hour with me dominating the conversation–the "teacher"–while my friends interjected only occasionally with a question of some sort, ever the gracious listeners. Eventually, the table next to us, which had been within earshot of our conversation all evening, got up to leave. As they were going, one of the women in their party stopped by my chair on her way out. Putting her hand firmly on my shoulder, she leaned in advisedly and informed me in no uncertain terms, "Honey, you're *not* an Introvert."

So it would seem.

INFJs, however, are fond of pointing out that very little about what we casually observe about people is what it seems, and almost never is this truer than INFJs being mistaken for Extraverts—a surprisingly common occurrence. So common, in fact, that I've practically come to *expect* disbelief and denial when friends and family learn that I'm an Introvert. More than any of the other Introverted personality types, INFJs are the ones most often confused for Extraverts it seems...Why?

Conventional wisdom posits that the telltale sign of an Extravert essentially lies in the exhibition of two "G's"—gregariousness and garrulousness. Sociability and talkativeness, respectively, are presumed to be the primary indicators of Extraversion. But this is a flawed interpretation of Jung's conception of Extraversion. While gregariousness and garrulousness frequently signify the dominance of Extraversion, they do not, by that fact alone, guarantee it. Similarly, a lack of one, or even both, of the two "G's" doesn't necessarily discount someone from being an Extravert either. Still, like so many of the more nuanced elements of typology that have been watered down, presumably to make typing easier and more accessible to the masses, the end result is more confusion than clarity. We'll return to the true nature of Extraversion and Introversion later, but first let's attempt to understand the phenomenon behind INFJs falsely being taken for Extraverts.

If there were only one function that most exemplifies gregariousness it would almost certainly be Extraverted Feeling (Fe). By its very nature, Fe is socially-oriented, with the "Feeling" component denoting its focus on people over things and the "Extraverted" component suggesting a gravitation to others while attracting them in kind; Fe types are quintessentially "people persons." Highly responsive to others, they are masters of emotional mirroring—the art of effortlessly conveying authenticity by exhibiting whatever sentiment happens to be dominating the group rapport.

Moreover, as a Judging function, Fe is usually just as comfortable taking the lead in facilitating group morale as it is being a mere participant. Intuitively gauging the social ease (or lack thereof) of a group, Fe types work to ensure affinity in social situations either by commanding action or using conversation to keep interpersonal dynamics running like a well-oiled machine. Because Extraverted Judging in combination with Feeling exhibits a kind of directness that seeks to exert influence over others, it has a magnifying effect, amplifying the perceived degree of Extraversion in Judgers over Perceivers even if the dominant function is technically Introverted as is the case for INFJs.

Still, as the first *Extraverted* function in their function stack, Fe is the primary way INFJs engage with the outside world. This means that Fe is also what others first encounter since dominant Ni is hidden from ready view as a result of its being Introverted in attitude. For this reason, when it comes to the strength of social affability granted by Fe, it could well be argued that IFJs are second only to EFJs with respect to "gregariousness." Stated alternately, INFJs tend to exhibit higher levels of Fe sociability than three-fourths of the types. Lenore Thomson, author of *Personality Type: An Owner's Manual*, puts it this way:

> *Because INFJs use Extraverted Feeling to relate to the outer world, they may seem more outgoing than they really are. Their personal approach and ability to find common ground with others...(means) they frequently find themselves in positions of authority.*[5]

But while it's one thing to be a "people person," or the kind of person who derives pleasure from being around others (something true of many Extraverts), it's entirely another to be a talkative, or garrulous, person. The act of talking (as opposed to the act of, well, *acting*) is one of giving expression to ideas symbolically, through language; and if action is chiefly the domain of Sensing, then language largely belongs to Intuition. This rule is particularly true any time the subject matter goes beyond the routine or pragmatic and into more theoretical and abstract matters. Therefore, should the topic of conversation land on one of INFJs' key interests such as psychology, spirituality, or interpersonal relations, INFJs can be inspired to get long-winded–precisely what our neighboring restaurant-goer was witnessing prior to lending her well-meaning however misguided insight.

For this reason, a strong Intuitive–even an Introverted one–can actually be more at home in conversation than many Sensing types. Indeed, among my aforementioned group of friends (an ESFP, ISFJ, INFP, and INFJ), the lone Extravert, the ESFP, is arguably the quietest of the bunch. Believe me when I say this *isn't* an anomaly. I've known and befriended many ESFPs over the course of my life and can say with a fair amount of confidence that I've out-talked them all!

In short, Ni and Fe in combination create what is arguably the *most outgoing* of the Introverted types in the form of INFJs–so much so that, as a child, despite my otherwise solid academic marks in school, the one critique I received without fail–year after year – was: "*Talks too much during class.*" Not exactly the kind of behavior one associates with Introversion. As an aside, when asked about it, my typical response was that I wasn't simply being a chatterbox but trying to "help other students understand the lesson"– presumptuous perhaps, but not necessarily unusual for an INFJ.

Hopefully, this sheds some light on the misunderstanding that commonly surrounds Introversion and Extraversion. The foundation of Introversion and Extraversion, from a Jungian perspective, is actually one of directionality with respect to energy (Extraversion tends to direct energy "outward" and Introversion "inward")–not the degree to which one is necessarily considered "outgoing." The specifics regarding *what* is directed outward or inward is ultimately dictated by the preferences (Feeling, Thinking, Intuition, or Sensing) in order to form the "functions," which of course vary by personality type. The lesson here is that, at the end of the day, it's just not as simple as saying that Extraverts are social and talkative or that Introverts are quiet and shy.

• • •

It could be argued that at the heart of the Introversion - Extraversion phenomenon is what essentially amounts to a theory of relativity. Extraverts tend to operate on the assumption that the so-called "outer world" is the primary (if not the only) reality that exists; it also happens to be the one in which they direct the majority of their energy. Introverts, by contrast, treat their inner world as the primary reality and prefer to direct their energy there first. They are both equally valid "worlds," but one is subjectively perceived as more real depending on whether the beholder is an Extravert or Introvert. Hence, it could be argued that with respect to the *inner* world, Introverts actually operate as Extraverts and, conversely, Extraverts as Introverts.

It may be appropriate to conceive Introversion and Extraversion as exactly that: two worlds existing on either side of a looking glass. Separated by a distinct yet penetrable veneer, one side is experienced as reality and the other as illusory depending on the world you presently inhabit. Yet these worlds are not quite so independent as they might seem, as what happens in one creates equal but opposite effects in the other. Furthermore, it can be almost impossible at times to tell where one world ends and the other begins. This means that occasionally we wander through to the other side, oblivious as to how or why, or even that we've done so at all.

It may come as no surprise that I was positively enamored with the story of Alice in Wonderland as a child–something that can hardly be considered a coincidence in retrospect. That story contained early lessons regarding our perceptions of reality–the incredibly frustrating experience of seeing things that others don't and the struggle to convince them of the truth as you know or experience it–all of which are central themes in the INFJ's life. Obviously, something in me found resonance with Alice's experience, even from early on. I think many INFJs can relate to the feeling that they've accidentally stumbled into a world in which they clearly experience themselves as outsiders.

The aforementioned happens because the Extraverted Sensing realities on the other side of the looking glass take on an unfamiliar and illusory quality when viewed from INFJs' usual perspective of Introverted Intuition. As a result, waking life feels like a dream and dreams feel very much like real life. Conversely, when INFJs wander back through the looking glass into the familiar homeland of Ni, there's a sense in which the INFJ has all but left "real" space and time to those in the outer Sensing world; from an Se vantage point, little about the INFJ's Ni world makes sense.

This is explainable by a key principle of type dynamics mentioned previously: when a psychological function emerges into consciousness, its paradoxical opposite reciprocally recedes into the unconscious. For INFJs, the strengthening of Ni in consciousness results in a weakening of Se. At the same time this is happening in consciousness, Ni is being weakened in the unconscious. This is a basic law of psychological cause and effect as it pertains to the conscious and unconscious minds: two worlds with equal but opposite actions and reactions occurring between them.

The resulting experience is that the material contained in the unconscious, should we encounter it, takes on a dream-like quality—powerful, fanciful, and full of distorted or exaggerated images which are often simplified yet hyperbolic. This is how the INFJ child experiences so-called "Sensing reality" in the outside world. Objects and experiences that seem perfectly benign to most Sensing children are frequently met with wide-eyed terror or wonder by Ni. By contrast, what feels truly "real" and trustworthy to the INFJ are the images and ideas flowing from the inner world of Intuition which, for them, are more easily managed than external reality.

These inner imaginings are the life-sustaining brio of INFJ children, and the resolute belief in the "realness" of their inner imaginings comes naturally to them (assuming they've been raised in a healthy environment and given permission to explore them freely). Of course, all children possess a strength of imagination; of that there's no doubt. Bouncing back and forth between reality and the imagination is the way that children begin making sense of things like Intuition and Sensing, and Introversion and Extraversion, in an attempt to differentiate the dominant function and kickstart the self-discovery process. But Extraverted Sensing types seem to get straight fairly early on when they're playing make-believe as opposed to truly believing the play they're making–INFJ children, by contrast, are often slower to catch on.

Unsurprisingly, INFJ children are typically comfortable engaging in autonomous, creative playtime for extended periods of time. An example from my own childhood: when I was around five years old my mother and her friend were visiting together in the living room for several hours when it dawned on her friend (an ESFJ) that it was well past lunchtime and I was still in my room playing. "Aren't you going to tell her to come out and eat??" She was distressed. My mother however, herself an INFJ and well-attuned to my nature, appeared nonplused. "Nah," she replied, "she'll come out when she's hungry." As an Intuitive, she seemed to understand what others types don't: obviously, when Ni is at work there's no time for unnecessary frivolities like eating and such.

Indeed, young INFJs may become so engrossed in their inner world that it leaves them blithely unaware of the external realities surrounding them, such as whether they're being watched or if their volume level is suitable to the environment. In these cases INFJs may be just as boisterous as Extraverted children, especially if they've managed to draw others into their imaginary world along with them. But this can shift as soon as the outside world is brought back into the INFJs' conscious awareness. Often, the expectation of Extraversion alone is enough to cause an about-face. It wouldn't be unusual, for example, to see an INFJ child, initially oblivious to being observed, playing around vociferously until suddenly being told to smile for the camera and abruptly turning coy.

For the most part, however, undifferentiated Ni (which is strongest in the first decade of life or so) is typically able to shut out or ignore any part of the outside world that isn't conducive to its aims. By remaining largely unencumbered by Se concerns, childhood development is dedicated to discovering and embracing

INFJs' natural preference for Ni, thus allowing them to stay immersed in a relatively pure dominant function state in which to be more authentic and carefree (something true of most children which explains why, given a healthy home life, we tend to romanticize early childhood).

• • •

Once the dominant function has been established, INFJs' auxiliary function, Extraverted Feeling, makes its appearance on the scene, nudging INFJs toward Extraversion in a more conscious way than before. A well-developed auxiliary function (in the opposite attitude from the dominant function) is necessary for healthy psychological development; otherwise, to quote Jung, we would all "end up in a lunatic asylum" (and I dare say INFJs would be among the first to go if they didn't.) I suspect that folks who resist being labeled a strict "Introvert" or "Extravert" are intuitively responding to this reality while failing to grasp the full scope of type as inclusive of *both* attitudes according to the function stack, but I digress.

The advent of the auxiliary function brings the promise of some sort of balance to the dominant function in that Introversion is now compensated by some amount of Extraversion (or vice-versa) and Perceiving by some amount of Judging (or vice-versa). Together, the dominant and auxiliary functions have a complementary effect, like a hero and his sidekick, better as a team than each on his own. As it happens, for many people, growth tends to stall or stagnate once they develop the auxiliary function since it confers "good enough" psychological functioning without the messiness of having to contend with the lower functions contained in the unconscious.

As the auxiliary function makes its way into consciousness, we undergo the psychological transformation known as "function differentiation." This is exactly what it sounds like: the act of consciously distinguishing, or differentiating, between the use of two different functions. Through this process, we are confronted with a new challenge as we become increasingly aware of psychological tension as a result of distinct forces vying, often in conflicting ways, for our time and energy.

Tension is the energy that simultaneously attracts and repels two forces, thereby binding them into a mutual relationship with one another. Ideally, we find a way to sync the tension of the dominant and auxiliary functions into a state of optimal union and symbiosis. This is most commonly experienced when the auxiliary function is being used as precisely that: something that is *auxiliary* to, or in the service of, the dominant function. The psyche, recognizing that the core self still finds its primary identity in the dominant function, is typically satisfied with such an arrangement; this is what we experience as *authenticity*.

If, however, the auxiliary function (or any of the lower functions for that matter) attempts to usurp power ahead of the dominant function, either by acting in opposition to it or commanding it into its employ, the relationship turns parasitic. We typically experience this perversion of power in the form of negative feelings associated with *inauthenticity*: inner tension or conflict, irritability, boredom, depression, anxiety, etc. As a rule, such a state is only sustainable for so long. Eventually, it becomes imperative to reinstate the dominant function to its rightful place so we can get back on track spiritually and psychologically.

For INFJs, the tension between the dominant and auxiliary functions involves the relationship between Ni and Fe. When Fe is primarily used as a support to Ni, as a means to convey and convince others of the importance of Ni's insights, INFJs experience an optimal state of symbiosis and authenticity. As long as this is the case, INFJs should be able to maintain a sufficient level of Extraversion without becoming drained, energy wise. But when Fe goes rogue by chiefly focusing on placating the emotional and physical needs of others without the benefit of deeper Ni insight, INFJs often find themselves on the path to burnout.

Indeed, it's not unusual for INFJs to appear incredibly outgoing and engaged in a social situation one minute, only to fall off the map the next. As Thomson keenly quips, "Such types are by turns highly sociable and maddeningly inaccessible." As it is, Fe, as a sort of permanent antenna attuned to other people, is simply too significant a part of INFJs' function stack–too hardwired into the system, if you will–to be turned off in social settings. For that reason, INFJs often feel that the only way to authentically block the possibility of incoming signals (i.e., social expectations) is to simply remove themselves from the physical environment altogether–often abruptly.

Never is this more true than when INFJs are of the belief–which is often–that their Intuitions will not be received with the kind of earnest appreciation and respect they believe they deserve. Unwilling to shun social obligations outright, they may feel forced to maintain more superficial relations with others until they can deploy the escape hatch and go back to their Intuitive solitude once more. Frequently, this back and forth becomes something of a dance for INFJs who get caught between two sides of the looking glass, keeping one foot in "Introvertland" and the other in "Extravertland," so to speak. That dance is a usually a sign that a "grip experience" may be just around the corner. Indeed, of all the potential triggers for falling into the grip (and there are many), the one that INFJs seem to cite most often is Fe burnout. Though, in theory, being forced to engage with functions lower in the stack, such as Ti and Se, should be more apt to induce a grip experience, the abuse of Fe always gets the lion's share of drum banging in INFJ circles. Why?

There are several possible reasons. First, because Fe retains a more conscious position in the function stack, INFJs may simply be more aware of when and how it's being used (or abused, for that matter.) Second, INFJs will often quickly rebuff any task related to Thinking and Sensing they find distasteful– balancing their checkbooks, handling car repairs, etc.–thus wisely avoiding their biggest triggers. On the other hand, because Fe is more difficult to authentically repress and is utilized more often, it provides more opportunities for INFJs to reach the point of burnout. Lastly, even when lower functions like Se are to blame, INFJs may be reluctant to admit it since renouncing the inferior function threatens to deny us wholeness.

INFJs attempting to defend the inferior function may forsake any personal responsibility for willingly engaging Se and instead project blame onto Fe, a convenient scapegoat since these two functions often go hand-in-hand. For example, an INFJ might willingly—even enthusiastically—agree to take on the task of baking and decorating three dozen cupcakes for a friend's birthday party—an opportunity to turn a creative Ni vision into an Se reality with the added bonus of meeting Fe needs. But halfway through, as the Sensing task becomes burdensome and frustration mounts toward a grip experience, rather than acknowledging that agreeing to the project may have been a bad idea, the INFJ vents resentment this way: "*I'm constantly giving myself to others! People are always taking advantage of me because they know I care about them and don't want to let them down!*"

Ironically, INFJs—usually good at reframing problems to find an inventive best-fit solution—are often unable in a grip state to see the obvious way out: simply order the cupcakes from a local bakery. Doing so would allow Fe's social responsibilities to remain intact without necessarily overburdening Se. Nevertheless, rather than acknowledging the unwise decision to commit to tackling a Sensing-heavy project personally rather than farm it out, the INFJ insists that the problems lies with the expectations of others and her Fe obligation to fulfill them.

To be fair, it's not always clear which particular function is responsible for a grip experience (it's often a blend) and INFJs pulled into doing favors for others, Sensing or otherwise, are simply doing their best to navigate the high-wire act of balancing social propriety with the need to conserve enough energy to fan their inner Ni flames—a difficult task for which they can incur considerable anxiety. Complicating matters is the fact that many of INFJs' expressions of Ni insight emerge freely and organically from Fe, giving others the impression that they are happy to take on a more helpful role in other areas such as Sensing tasks. Over time, people may come to expect INFJs to provide a level of Extraversion disproportionate to their authentic preference. This creates a dilemma for INFJs who, feeling an obligation not to disappoint, put on a stronger Fe act than is truly authentic, thus creating a vicious cycle.

This often saddles INFJs with more external responsibility than they can authentically manage as Introverts. Where ENFJs and ESFJs tend to thrive on this sort of calling, INFJs tend to feel conflicted over how much time to authentically devote to others versus pursuing their own Ni interests. Lenore Thomson insightfully captures this reality:

> *(INFJs') primary relationship is to their inner world, and they are receptive to others only up to a point. Indeed, these types often find that their sympathy and perceptive listening have been mistaken for an overture of friendship, which they didn't intend...The truth is that Introverted Intuition inclines them to keep a part of themselves in reserve–to locate their true identity outside the expectations and definitions of others.*[6]

So what exactly is this part of themselves that INFJs are keeping in reserve, their so-called "true identity?" Here's a hint: it's not their personal feelings.

This brings another opportunity to highlight a key difference between INFJs and INFPs. For INFPs, the part of themselves being held in reserve is the powerful spectrum of inner emotions represented by Introverted Feeling (Fi)–joy, love, anger, sadness, pain, etc.–which they tend to share only with their most trusted intimates, if at all. The INFP's outward demeanor, typically cool and calm, often belies the hurricane of emotions swirling around in them internally. An excellent example of this comes from the movie *The Philadelphia Story* wherein Jimmy Stewart's character gives a bang-on description of Katharine Hepburn's inner Fi nature despite her outwardly icy demeanor, saying, "*You're lit from within, Tracy. You've got fires banked down in you, hearth-fires and holocausts.*" INFPs surely resonate with possessing this inner tempest.

Too often however, these sorts of inner, personal emotions are conflated with Ni in INFJs. The truth is, personal feelings are not nearly as hallowed for INFJs as they are for INFPs. Because INFJs experience Feeling in the Extraverted attitude (Fe), they are more overtly expressive with emotional displays, not necessarily holding what you might consider a "deep personal attachment" to them. That reality is often written all over the face of INFJs via dramatic eyebrow movements, sweeping smiles, overt grimaces, and gratuitous head-noddings. It's also witnessed in the passionate and melodic timbre of their voices (not exactly monotonal) thanks to Fe's penchant for covering the entire range of notes on the emotional spectrum–often in a single sentence.

• • •

More than their personal feelings, what's most sacred to INFJs is the working theories roiling around in Ni–the earliest origins of insight that explain our experiences. In truth, it's far more accurate to call them insights–or visions–than "feelings." These visions are the inner Intuitive contents that INFJs safeguard most vigilantly, away from prying, skeptical eyes.

INFJs can be especially protective of their solitude in the earliest stages of Ni, when the message being relayed is but a subtle whisper, requiring INFJs to strain harder than usual to hear what the Intuitive universe is trying to tell them. Like a faint flicker in a sea of fog, if INFJs get distracted or fail to move in almost immediately, there's a sense that they risk losing that little bit of light to obscurity's expanse forever. To avoid being eluded, INFJs feel they have to block any interference from the outside world; it's the only way to know whether they're dealing with a spark or a supernova.

How Ni actually reveals itself, or relays its message, is arguably the least describable and most ineffable part of INFJs' experience since that's exactly what Intuition is: an abstract conception for which INFJs continually seek concrete definition. Frequently described as a "vision" or "insight," Ni is probably best understood as a kind of perspective–a way of looking at a familiar object from an entirely different angle such that it reveals something totally new, despite having existed all along.

As a child of the 90's, I remember seeing a Magic Eye stereogram for the very first time, which were all the rage then. I was completely awestruck when, after staring at a flat plane of simple dots and waves, a 3-D world of underwater sea life–fish, dolphins, and seaweed–suddenly emerged as if from out of nowhere. *Incredible! Where had it come from?* This is an excellent illustration of what Ni is like: it's the experience of watching a hidden universe reveal itself to you, as if by magic, from inside or behind the supposedly more "real" or obvious one. As an aside, what amused me at the time was how long some of the adults stood there staring at it, confounded and shaking their heads every thirty seconds or so while muttering, "*I just don't see it...*"–an early lesson in the first commandment of Ni, which posits that just because someone else can't see something doesn't mean it doesn't exist.

Another way of understanding the experience of seeing things through an Ni lens is that, when it comes to the text of life, INFJs are of the firm conviction that behind every message clearly printed in black and white lies a hidden one marked with a kind of invisible ink; where most people are initially seeing the "obvious" black and white one, the latent message is what paradoxically seems to reveal itself most clearly to Ni. In other words, where other personality types are apparently reading plain text, INFJs are reading *subtext.* Indeed, it's helpful to think of Se and Ni as two types of text–plain text and subtext. Where most people read the plain text first and *then* infer the deeper meaning, INFJs work the other way by using the hidden message to decode the one in plain text–a practice that is a lot like trying to reconstruct the details of a story's plotline using nothing but the footnotes and commentary.

But to say the hidden messages contained by Ni reveal themselves all at once, fully formed and in vivid detail, would be a bit misleading. Rather, these intuitions often arise as faint impressions–as pieces of shape and bits of line–making it possible to know that *something* is there, but not always *what* exactly. In truth, INFJs usually have to work a bit harder if they wish to flesh out the full picture. The satisfaction of elaboration is often only achievable once INFJs have incorporated some manner of Judging into the Perceiving process–usually through the use of symbolic language. The result is what most consider to be the INFJ's bread and butter: metaphor and simile.

If it wasn't already evident, INFJs are enthusiastic employers of the metaphor; it's how they attempt to bridge the subtext of conceptual Intuition back to the plain text of Sensory experience. David Keirsey elaborates on this tendency saying,

> *(INFJs) use an unusual degree of imagery in their language, the kind of imagery found in complex and often aesthetic writing such as novels, plays, and poems... In all their communications they are masters of the metaphor, and will naturally describe a thing in terms of something else.*[7]

Employing symbolic language to effectively "paint with words," INFJs work to translate Ni's message in a way that is relatable to Sensing experience but also retains the profundity of the original meaning. The end result is a meticulously crafted metaphor: each artfully selected word a sweeping pass of nacre coating the coarse seed of early Intuition. And it's often only after polishing their product in isolation that INFJs will consider revealing it to the outside world. Once again we turn to Lenore Thomson:

> *IN(F)Js are least accessible in the discovery process period. Like the prince in the story of Cinderella, they're solitary, sometimes obsessive, fitting Intuition to expressible terms like the glass slipper to potential brides. Until they've managed a good enough fit, between their inner reality and an outward vocabulary, IN(F)Js may not even know what they're after, and they won't involve others in formulating their plans.*[8]

Keeping unwanted external interruptions at bay isn't simply aimed at shutting out social obligations brought on by Fe. As an Introverted function, Ni is typically unreceptive to information foisted on them from the outside world as well (e.g., Extraverted Intuition). Interestingly, intrusions from Extraverted Intuition (Ne) can actually be *more* disruptive to the Ni process than those coming from Fe. This presents a real challenge at times since many of INFJs' nearest and dearest are NP types. Even still, it's not at all unusual to see a clash of Ni and Ne wills, especially early in INFJs' Intuitive process.

The resistance to interference from Ne is threefold. First, because the only way INFJs can experience authentic knowing is if inner Intuition leads them to it independently, being beaten to the punch by Ne types with their pre-acquired knowledge robs INFJs of the opportunity to "know" things with deep and abiding conviction for themselves. While Ne research obtained after the fact is perfectly acceptable, welcomed even, as an affirmation of Ni "knowing," this is only true once Ni has been allowed to work through its theories on its own. This can be difficult for Ne types to grasp since it runs counter to their view that virtually all conceptual knowledge is acquired from without.

INFJs who fail to do their preliminary Ne research are often looked upon with great skepticism by NPs, leading to the second source of resistance at sharing their early intuitions: Ne doubt. NPs' propensity for intellectual "gun-jumping," where pre-acquired knowledge is used to cut short budding insights from Ni, has already been established. But what if Ni manages to unearth a virgin insight as yet undiscovered by Ne? Lacking a sufficient supply of outside references, Ni's early theories are often met with a swift and healthy dose of skepticism by NPs, at first blush anyway. As far as NPs are concerned, INFJs may as well have pulled this stuff right out of their, well...*you know*. This kind of discouragement can be especially demoralizing for INFJs whose Fe can be sensitive to others' input, leading many to simply throw in the towel on their Ni efforts.

Lastly, even if their theories do manage to outrun the aforementioned challenges, an entirely different obstacle awaits INFJs at the end of the Ne gauntlet: what I like to call "insight-napping." Every so often, NPs catch wind of an Ni insight that piques their interest and makes their heart go all pitter patter. We can't exactly blame them–latching onto new ideas is what Ne types do best, afterall. Still, INFJs unwilling to have the unripened fruits of their labor picked prematurely can become fiercely protective if they sense NPs approaching excitedly with sticky fingers. Understandably cautious, INFJs may wisely block them out until they've had time to bring their insights to their full developmental potential.

Ironically however, the same Ne winds with the power to snuff out Ni's intuitive flame also have the potential to fan it into a full-blown blaze eventually, but INFJs must be allowed to stoke the embers of their own insights long enough to ensure the latter outcome. The main problem, thematically, in the aforementioned cases involves the readiness of INFJs' intuitions to come out of isolative incubation, or Introversion, before their time. If shared too early, Ni's intuitions might never have a chance to get off the ground, but NPs entering the scene at just the right moment may actually be INFJs' best hope for disseminating their Ni insights. For that reason, when it comes to how INFJs should include NPs in their Ni process, it really is a case of the old adage, "timing is everything."

INFJs know, at least subconsciously, that insights nurtured in Ni's womb for as long as possible stand a lesser chance of being misconstrued–or, worse, rejected outright–once they reach the outside world. It's in this early phase of research and development, behind closed doors, that they retain almost exclusive control, after which they have little to no way of controlling the pyres they've wrought. INFJs' primary job, then, is to carefully cultivate their insights and theories *in shell* with sufficient clarity, proof and justification before being harvested lest their Intuitive efforts–and *raison d'etre*–be for naught.

3. RELATIONSHIPS (n. pl.)

"He was a bold man that first ate an oyster."

Jonathan Swift

Consistent with INFJs' belief that outward experience is intimately connected to and reflective of a deeper reality, relationships are not just relationships to INFJs, but represent something more complex: the symbolic potential to successfully transcend oneself and achieve unification with the larger Self. In this way, a successful relationship—whether professional, friendship, or romantic—can be an almost spiritual experience, creating pathways of connection and understanding that enable parties to broaden the scope of any individual ego, toward a model of growth and wholeness. And while INFJs certainly seek entertainment and enjoyment from their relationships, shared experiences alone typically don't form the foundation of what INFJs consider truly worthwhile about relationships.

Instead, INFJs see relationships as *pathways to actualization*, both for themselves and others. I emphasize this point because it's helpful for those seeking to understand how INFJs approach relationships—in fact, it is probably one of the most important things that others working to build a relationship with INFJs can know about them. From INFJs' perspective, it's possible to raise the value of one's individual experience (to transcend ego consciousness, in other words) by working within a relational context to explore and realize Ni's insights in concert with others. Indeed, for INFJs, it's not just possible, but imperative.

Much as ISFJs are seen as guardians of knowledge with respect to traditions ("traditions" being the behavioral patterns and rituals that have historically ensured social cohesion and cooperation as a meaningful part of the collective human experience), INFJs are also guardians of a sort. But instead of being guardians of tradition, they function as guardians of "spiritual insight," namely, knowledge which brings psychological salubrity and symbolic meaning to the human experience. It's this knowledge that INFJs are continually striving to impart and preserve in their interactions with others.

Due to INFJs' unusually high expectation of a shared metaphysical connection, truly meaningful relationships are typically not as plentiful or easily made as they are for say, Extraverted Sensing types. Where other personality types tend to qualify their friendships on the basis of things like common interests, shared activities, or even mere proximity (neighbors and co-workers, for example), INFJs crave friendships based on something deeper: intellectual and emotional compatibility. Relationships founded on "doing things" rather than "talking about things" generally strike INFJs as somewhat hollow or empty. Ultimately, INFJs aren't so much seeking playmates as they are *soul* mates.

That said, most INFJs don't expect perfect compatibility right out of the gate. What they are primarily looking for is the *potential* for intellectual and spiritual compatibility which, in time, might approach something that transcends ordinary experience. The high value they place on potential in their relationships is one reason ending relationships can be incredibly difficult and painful for INFJs. Even when the reality of a relationship proves disappointing, their conviction regarding its intuited potential makes letting go almost impossible.

As a result of the high value they place on their relationships, INFJs tend to be somewhat selective on the front end of them, waiting to invest a significant commitment of time and energy until they've gathered enough information from Ni regarding others' ability to have a more meaningful relationship. Fortunately, INFJs are well-equipped to sniff out potential in others, including identifying "diamonds in the rough" relationship wise.

So what does an INFJ recognize as "potential" in a relationship? Two qualities top the list: a lack of ego defensiveness and a desire for greater consciousness. This requires being firmly committed to the higher Self while being unattached to the comfort afforded by ignorance of one's ego defenses. Simply, INFJs are seeking authenticity and openness. The cornerstone of any meaningful INFJ relationship, then, is a willingness to embrace honesty and to invest in the relationship, even in times of difficulty. This is why INFJs typically make friends–at least the close ones–for life.

Ironically, even with the aid of perspicacity provided by Ni, young and unlearned INFJs may suffer from the same short-sightedness as others by assuming that the rest of the world values the same things they do. Like most Judging types, they are *generalizers* by nature, and they're not immune from the trappings of projection. It's therefore not uncommon for younger INFJs to assume that the insight into the unconscious they seek is similarly desired by others.

That assumption, paired with Judging from auxiliary Fe, can compel INFJs to boldly proclaim their observations and insights unsolicited–including the harsher ones. Unsurprisingly, this tends to land young INFJs in a heap of trouble, particularly with their Sensing superiors who view such behavior as not just disruptive but downright impertinent. While there may be considerable truth in the trenchant remarks of young INFJs still learning the art of diplomacy, that's arguably what makes them so brazen from the perspective of their Sensing elders–their prescience.

Such conflicts also occur because INFJs are instinctively operating from a different set of rules than the Sensing establishment. From INFJs' perspective, it's not physical age that necessarily merits respect (a Sensing "rule of thumb"), but one's *psychospiritual* age; and INFJs are keenly aware that physical age is not always indicative of psychospiritual age. The fact is, even young INFJs can be incredibly sensitive to acts of ego defensiveness and inauthenticity: telltale signs of spiritual immaturity under Ni's watchful eye. They are often quick to call out hypocrisy or moral turpitude wherever they see it, irrespective of the consequences.

It's essential to highlight this behavior as *a phase* of development, not a persistent trait of well-developed INFJs. To be fair, INFJs are no more immune to the rocky process of individuation than any other type. Like a novice gymnast on the balance beam, there are early periods of flailing and overcorrection that take place before equilibrium is achieved. It can take years before INFJs realize that ramrodding their perceptions down others' throats is rarely effective; indeed, it often makes things worse. In truth, however, INFJs aren't likely to change their outspoken ways for those they don't respect anyway. Sadly, it often takes the destruction of at least one relationship that truly matters, and sometimes more, before they finally see the light.

• • •

So, what kind of person or personality type might be up to tackling a relationship with an INFJ?

In many cases, the psychological function most willing to take on Ni is its directional opposite, Extraverted Intuition. Ne types, with their openness to pretty much anything, are among the few willing to entertain some of Ni's more radical insights. NPs also tend to be effective messengers and disseminators of information. For this reason, they're veritable godsends for INFJs who view their advent as bringing the promise of actualization. "Finally!" the INFJ rejoices, "Someone has come with a bucket to fetch water from my Ni well!" It's why, in almost every religious text, beside every INFJ prophet is at least one NP disciple.

NPs' mere openness to Ni is often enough to kindle the INFJ's interest and trust in them–an invitation to divulge increasingly provocative advice and insight. Indeed, it's not unusual for NPs to display not just openness, but genuine enthusiasm during their first few brushes with Ni. As a result, INFJs, believing NPs to be up to the task of bearing growth-related insights, will often push them as hard as possible in hopes of spurring some sort of spiritual transformation.

This may be well and good for a time, but it's rarely long before INFJs manage to push their open-minded companions one step too far. Frustrated from being hammered relentlessly about the ways they're falling short (the implication of which is nothing they do is ever good enough), it's not unusual for them to rail against the INFJ eventually; even NPs have their limits! This can catch INFJs by surprise, however, since they see pushing their NP companions as an indication of their respect and faith in them. Afterall, why bother investing so much time and energy in someone, the INFJ figures, if he or she didn't show great promise?

Unfortunately, by the time things reach this point, such arguments typically fall on deaf ears, which is entirely understandable. NPs simply grow weary of feeling more like "projects" than friends. What's more, the sudden blowback from NPs is often met poorly by INFJs, causing NPs to accuse INFJs of "dishing it out" but unable to take it in kind. That sort of double standard doesn't sit well with NPs, providing them with another reason to potentially cut ties with the INFJ.

Impartial analysis suggests that NPs' allegations are usually justified. Often, without even realizing it, INFJs pull a subtle switcheroo on their companions by not merely conveying insight or advice, but becoming increasingly consumed with its manifestation in their lives. The effective result is that INFJs are no longer just playing witness to friends and family, but judge and jury as well. Particularly where an insight into personal growth has already been brought to light, INFJs have a rather bad habit of policing their friends and partners for any act perceived to be in violation of their higher Self. As such, it's easy for INFJs to unwittingly morph into the over-interested managers of others' lives.

• • •

NP types aren't the only ones subject to this kind of psychospiritual supervision from INFJs. A common grievance generally among INFJs' friends and family involves INFJs' perpetual complaining about others' lack of self-awareness. *Can't we simply enjoy spending time together without subjecting every last action to analysis and scrutiny,* friends and family wonder, *or must every interaction involve some sort of lesson in morality?* As a result, INFJs can earn a reputation for being real social downers or buzzkills, and they may find others pulling away in attempt to avoid being exposed to constant psychoanalysis and critique.

Any time Extraverted Judging takes over and INFJs veer into "management" mode, they can resemble ENFJ types with whom they share all the same typological functions, only in a slightly different order. Having all but abandoned Ni, INFJs' primary focus becomes exacting moral order and compliance in those around them by way of Extraverted Feeling. This warrants consideration of Lenore Thomson's remarks on Extraverted Feeling types (EFJs) because of its relevance to INFJs as well:

> *Such types consider themselves authorities on human relationship, and they're always ready to tell others how to live their lives. Fearing that people aren't as strong or as logical as they are, their advice is often unsolicited, intended to keep people from making bad decisions... Such types believe they're taking action on behalf of others, but they're increasingly stubborn about getting their own way. They don't recognize they're deciding for others, limiting people's opportunities to take responsibility for themselves.*[9]

With respect to the subsequent resentment FJs feel when others fail to heed their advice, Thomson continues:

> *(EFJs) feel mistreated because others won't conform to their unrealistic expectations... (but) they aren't taking people's individual needs and experience into account.*[10]

Often, it's only after INFJs manage to turn the mirror they've subjected others to onto themselves, by scrutinizing their *own* subconscious motivations, that they see any real improvement in how others respond to them.

But this is easier said than done; how does a mirror go about reflecting itself? Indeed, for all of their powers of perception into others, INFJs can exhibit a surprising lack of self-awareness as a result of weak Introverted Judging which is located further down in the function stack. A rather unflattering truth about INFJs is it's often far too easy for them to focus on bringing their partners, friends, and family into psychic maturity while ignoring almost entirely their own psychospiritual shortcomings. Again, Thomson is on point:

> *INFJs are... capable of surrounding themselves with people whose Judgment skills are undeveloped, which gives them the opportunity to conduct their relationships by advising others on the wisdom of their life choices...It takes a deliberate effort for INFJs to use their Judgment for self-criticism, and not just to analyze the limits of others' ideas. Until they learn to do this, they're nearly impervious to criticism from anyone. Even INFJs, who can be seriously wounded by a rift in a relationships, are unlikely to take another's opinion of them at face value.*[11]

Much of this can be better understood in light of INFJs' propensity to take on a classic relational role commonly known in psychology circles as the "maximizer." Maximizers are distinguished by strong outer displays of feeling, hyperfocus on and assertiveness in their relationships, desire for mutual interdependence, and a need to be needed. They're relational "fighters" more than "flighters," "pursuers" as opposed to "the pursued." As a rule, maximizers tend to invest heavily in their relationships, preferring to address conflicts head on, often pushing their loved ones to lay their feelings on the line alongside them.

Like ENFJs, INFJs are naturally drawn to the maximizer role–another telltale difference between them and INFPs, who more commonly identify as "minimizers," or the "yin" to the maximizer's "yang." In contrast to maximizers, minimizers tend to be more withdrawn and self-contained, preferring to downplay their feelings and avoid conflict whenever possible. Although minimizers may hold strong feelings internally (especially IFPs), these are rarely given direct outward expression in a way that fully conveys their felt intensity. (I say "direct" because IFPs may–and often do–*indirectly* express their feelings via poetry, music, art, etc., but this is distinguished from the kind of face-to face, verbal confrontation directed at the object of one's feelings, which is more common among maximizers.) Not wanting to seem pushy or domineering, minimizers tend to recoil at the idea of being overly assertive and can appear dodgy or evasive when approached by maximizers in this way.

It probably goes without saying that minimizers and maximizers engage with each other in ways that are at once complementary and conflicting. This inspires a fairly predictable pattern of engagement wherein the more a minimizer withdraws, or "minimizes," the more the maximizer attempts to go after him or her (i.e., "maximizes"). Conversely, the more a maximizer "maximizes," the more the minimizer withdraws. As may be obvious, minimizers tend to have a stronger internal locus of control and maximizers a more robust external locus of control, meaning that most of the relational energy and focus tends to land on the minimizer (i.e., *not* the INFJ).

As explained previously, this disparity can beget conflict as minimizers lose patience with being relentlessly hounded by INFJ maximizers. The relationship often grows increasingly strained as long as INFJs are unable or unwilling to shift from Extraverted Judging (maximizing) toward Introverted Judging (minimizing). At this point, INFJs would be wise to consider how they themselves need to change rather than always assuming the onus is on the other person to change.

Ideally, INFJs would be able to execute the kind of self-awareness that would lead to a rebalancing of energy without necessarily putting their relationship at risk of a breakdown first. Unfortunately, absent a relational rift, a shift from Extraverted Judging (Fe) to Introverted Judging (Ti) often proves difficult for INFJs since Fe precedes Ti in their function stack. Sometimes it's only within the context of a failing relationship that INFJs can be persuaded to move into Introverted Judging where it then becomes easier to exact the inner resolve required to change.

Of course, as long as things are going well relationally, INFJs have little reason to question their methods. It's only when the relationships they hold dear begin to crumble that INFJs reach a pivotal point where they must decide whether to continue projecting blame onto others versus taking a hard look at themselves. Problematically, INFJs who sense that others are recoiling will often crank up the volume on Fe, dishing out increasingly more judgments until they've all but driven their loved ones away.

But before we judge INFJs too harshly, let's remember that this is how the learning curve of personal growth works for pretty much everyone: as a series of trial-of-error experiences. If the only tool we know how to use is a hammer, our instinct is to go around hammering things, even when a wrench is better suited to the task at hand. As long as a hammer gets the job done however, there's little incentive to seek out a different tool. As it is, real psychological and spiritual growth often occurs only when we meet resistance or experience "failure" since it forces us to consider engaging a new function, or "tool," in need of development.

Therefore, as long as INFJs can see a sliver of daylight in the doorway of their relationships, they will typically persist with their

Fe tactics, projecting and pushing expectations onto their loved ones while feeling powerless to change themselves. Again, even as their relationships grow increasingly strained, many will double-down on this approach, stubbornly concentrating all of their attention on the other person's need to change. Alas, INFJs do end up pushing others to act alright—usually by slamming the door to the relationship firmly in the INFJ's face.

It's usually at this point, with nothing but the shattered pieces of the relationship and no path to resolution through Fe, that INFJs realize they have nowhere left to turn but inward. And so it's often in this painful way that they are forced to examine their own role in relational breakdown, to question the efficacy of their methods, and to get to the bottom of where things went off the rails exactly.

While it may be tempting for INFJs to delude themselves into believing that their frustration with others is entirely justified—or, worse, their self-pity when they find themselves being shut out—choosing this path sets them up for a déjà vu of disappointment the next time it happens (and without some sort of paradigm shift, it almost certainly *will* happen again). Such delusions are born from INFJs' mistaken belief that their only motive has been to help bring others to psychospiritual awareness—*an altruistic aim, if there ever was one*, INFJs reason—leaving themselves blameless in the matter.

On closer inspection however, INFJs are likely to discover a fair bit of self-interest masquerading as altruism. One reason for this behavior is, deep down, INFJs fear that they can only be valuable if there's a psychospiritual problem that needs solving or when others are at a point of crisis and in need of their counsel. Indeed, INFJs may not know their value in a relationship beyond their ability to provide counsel or "fix" any problems therein. Uncertain as to what others find valuable about them exactly, INFJs may feel at a loss regarding their role in a relationship without some sort of issue to resolve—a reality they may not be consciously aware of.

If it strikes readers as curious that INFJs need a "role" in their relationships at all, they're not alone; such readers are likely operating from an Fi perspective. For Fi types, a person's value (in a relationship or otherwise) is inherent or self-evident—a "given." But Fe worth is measured by a different, if somewhat superficial, metric, one that sees value as something largely "bestowed" upon an individual, earned by virtue of one's utility to others and society. As an Extraverted function, Fe tends to view value through a collective or interpersonal lens—something arrived at more democratically than autocratically. In other words, Fe value is essentially *dependent* in nature.

For this reason, those with a prominent Fe function, like INFJs, have a fundamental need to be needed, to know their utility to others, and for others to know it too. By constantly pointing out others' shortcomings, INFJs may effectively be finding reasons to offer their counsel so that others continue to regard them as valuable in the relationship. And the ante is upped substantially whenever INFJs put their own personal feelings on the line by investing in a close friendship or romantic relationship. As a result, the more valuable the relationship to INFJs, the more vociferous and critical they may become.

The irony, of course, is that continually pointing out others' shortcomings usually results in frustration and resentment instead of appreciation and desire—the exact opposite reaction INFJs are attempting to bring about. Friends and family entreating them to refrain from endlessly critical psychoanalysis may try to convince INFJs that they value them for other aspects of their personality, like their fun and playful side. But because INFJs typically don't center their identity on those qualities, such entreaties are regularly dismissed, or even interpreted as insults, since they suggest that the other party doesn't really love and accept the INFJ for his or her "real self": Ni's insight-providing side.

In order to steer clear of the problems described above, it's advisable for INFJs to avoid appointing themselves as the designated counselors in their relationships, since doing so represents a profound conflict of interest, particularly for less self-aware INFJs. While it's one thing to provide counsel to a friend or partner as it pertains to *another* relationship (someone's co-worker, boss, outside friend, etc.), it's often too difficult for INFJs to check their subconscious motivations at the door or to guarantee objectivity when it comes to critiquing relationships in which they themselves are an intimate party.

One way for INFJs to effectively combat the temptation to play therapist in their relationships is to ensure that their Ni skills are being meaningfully employed *outside* their relationships on a regular basis (e.g., in a profession or career that channels their talents as counselors and insight providers). Often, INFJs unhappy in their day jobs as a result of their dominant and auxiliary functions not being engaged will subconsciously seek out ways to employ those functions in their "off-hours" (read: with friends and family). Those who are challenged and validated in careers that engage their strengths on a consistent basis, however, will usually feel fulfilled enough to resist the temptation to regularly "go to work" on their loved ones.

• • •

While the above may seem rather obvious, dealing as it does with the dominant and auxiliary functions, there is another, somewhat more obscure, factor driving INFJs' tendency to be critical in their relationships: the inferior function. Any time INFJs blame others for failing to heed their advice, they may be overlooking a blindspot with respect to their own unconscious motivations. INFJs who are honest with themselves will recognize that a major culprit behind their relational downfalls is not so much others' psychospiritual fallibility (which is, quite frankly, to be expected), but rather the unyielding way in which they've tried to *force* their loved ones to change to fit their vision of ideal behavior.

The most obvious offender, which has already been discussed, is Fe–its aggressive Judging attributes commonly cited by others as the source of their discontent. Because an unrefined Fe presents with the exasperation of a frustrated taskmaster more than the gentle patience of a horse whisperer, were INFJs to focus their efforts on softening the harsh edges of their judgments, parsing advice with greater finesse and scaling back their lectures accordingly, the reaction from friends and family would arguably be more favorable. But for INFJs to *solely* concentrate their efforts here is somewhat misguided. Like tossing water out of a leaky boat, trying to contain Fe is a never-ending battle that wrongly assumes the best solution is removing the water instead of patching the leak.

In other words, unbridled Fe might not, in fact, be the source of INFJs' interpersonal problems, but rather a symptom of something more insidious. The real cause of Fe stringency may be the rising discontent that has crept in, essentially unnoticed, by way of INFJs' inferior function, Extraverted Sensing. Subconscious Se expects–nay, demands–a certain degree of idealism in its experiences and material outcomes. It's this expectation that subtly, yet persistently, prompts Fe to execute Se's orders, even if it costs INFJs dearly in terms of interpersonal harmony. This illustrates how cleverly the inferior function manages to sneak into INFJs' dealings, effectively undermining the honest aims of Ni and Fe.

In truth, it's unlikely that Fe would go to such extremes in Judging–the kind of extremes that push people to slam shut the door of their relationships with the INFJ–if there wasn't so much riding on inferior Se. For this reason, tackling the inferior function problem (something that will be address in later chapters) has the added bonus of resolving many of Fe's issues as well.

For most INFJs however, the extreme discomfort involved with confronting the inferior function prompts them to continue using the same, familiar functions to navigate whatever challenges they're facing. Assuming they can empty water out of a leaky boat fast enough to keep their relationships afloat, they may be able to avoid confronting their inferior function issues for at least a little while–though usually not without some difficulty. With the true source of the problem left unaddressed, INFJs are forced to exercise major self-restraint as unmet inferior function expectations increase their desperation to use the very Fe tactics they're prohibited from employing due to the risks they pose to the relationship. But developing self-restraint is exactly the sort of strengthening exercise that can help INFJs develop their Introverted Judging function, Ti, prompting self-growth.

It's largely from this place of managing Fe/Ti "well enough"–by conveying concerns about others in a way that doesn't offend, while inwardly fending off the impulse to be more critical–that INFJs spend much of their lives. This is especially true in situations where they've already suffered the loss of a valuable relationship and have thus come to terms with the necessity of keeping their more critical judgments to themselves. It's possible that such experiences help INFJs build enough inner fortitude to accept the role of the ill-fated "go-between," finding a sort of purpose in learning how to bear that cross with increasing resilience.

• • •

None of the above is intended to diminish the profound and often selfless ways in which INFJs rise to meet the demands of their relationships. It should never be doubted that *relationships matter* to INFJs, and they invest heavily in them as a matter of principle. Indeed, it might be said that INFJs make careers out of being in relationships–expecting much, yes, but giving as much or more in return. Generous by nature, there is little an INFJ won't do to help a friend in need–even giving of their lower functions to the point of burnout, as illustrated in the previous chapter, if that's what's required to be of service.

At their most inspired, INFJs are seeing and encouraging the very best in the people they know and love, reinforcing their limitless potential with respect to personal growth, particularly where others struggle to see it for themselves. However, as INFJs are keenly aware, this is only possible once the ego has stepped aside enough to make way for the greater Self to emerge. And while it may be tempting for INFJs to give others' egos a little, shall we say, "*nudge,*" in order to help them realize their potential, this can have the unfortunate effect of backfiring on INFJs and the relationship as a whole.

Wiser INFJs have learned that the universe has a way of bringing people to the necessary psychospiritual crossroads with or without their help, and, as a rule, they would do better to let *it* decide on the ideal timing–when confronting the unconscious is apt to be maximally beneficial to the individual concerned–instead of attempting to take matters into their own hands. If and when the universe brings others to such a crossroad, INFJs can be there to provide *solicited* insight and advice, but they needn't sell others on their value to them before it's time.

4. SECURITY (n.)

"The eldest oyster winked his eye,
And shook his heavy head–
Meaning to say he did not choose
To leave the oyster-bed."

Lewis Carroll

I was about four years old. My grandparents had decided to take the grandkids to a nearby theme park in Williamsburg one stifling summer day and, passing through the entry gates, the sense of anticipation that filled the air was as thick as the sticky Virginia heat. It was my first time at this particular amusement park and I had no idea what to expect. Making our way through the crowd, the first ride we approached–a kiddie-style attraction with brightly colored sailboats floating innocently around a little lagoon–was instantly met with wide-eyed terror as I assessed the situation through INFJ lenses: *It could be a death trap.*

Sensing my reticence, my grandmother gently prompted me into the queue, "Go on honey, it's perfectly safe..." I wasn't convinced. As we approached the loading dock, I froze up in fear as she attempted to urge me forward yet again, "It's okay dear, go ahead." Not to be taken for a fool, I did what any precocious INFJ would do: I offered up my similarly-aged cousin to sacrificially tempt fate. "Let *him* go first," was my leery rejoinder, eyes askance. This was amusing on its own, but what followed cemented the comedy of personality dynamics at play as my cousin, an Extravert, obliged the request without the slightest hesitation, shrugging nonchalantly and muttering, "okee-dokee!" as he blithely boarded the boat, hilariously true to Extraverted form. Poor guy. I'm pretty sure it took him two or three trips around the lagoon unaccompanied before I determined that it was "probably" safe for me to ride as well.

As my little anecdote illustrates, confronting the great big Sensing world directly can be an overwhelming experience for INFJs–particularly in childhood. INFJs' tentativeness toward the environment can be traced, theoretically, to the time when Introverted Intuition begins to emerge as the dominant function. That's because as Ni grows in consciousness, its paradoxical partner, Extraverted Sensing, recedes into the unconscious where it remains until, at some point in early adulthood, INFJs begin the arduous task of trying to integrate it back into consciousness.

Early on however, as Ni works to differentiate itself from Se, INFJs lose touch with the hard realities supplied by the five senses: the result of repressing Sensing. As Ni grows in strength and prominence, Se fades into the background, like a dream that largely goes ignored by INFJs. Small changes in the environment that don't directly impact the INFJ's internal stasis are unlikely to be registered into consciousness, establishing a pattern in which INFJs repress Se as a way of life. The clever subconscious, recognizing the weakening of Sensing perception, grows increasingly wary of the environment, casting doubt on the trustworthiness of the five senses.

What follows is a sort of self-fulfilling prophecy in which anything pertaining to Sensing is avoided out of the fear that it cannot be effectively managed, and this results in the continued weakening of Sensing which reinforces INFJs' fear regarding their inability to control Se circumstances, thus perpetuating the cycle. Eventually, the Sensing process becomes so anemic and fragile that it takes on the distorted and exaggerated qualities associated with the inferior function generally. In the eyes of INFJ children, this skewed perception of Se reality can make positive experiences, like opening Christmas presents or taking a trip to Disneyland, positively awe-inspiring; but conversely, it can also make more intimidating experiences, like learning to swim or going to the dentist, absolutely terrifying.

The relative "dysfunction" of Se in young INFJs may go largely unnoticed or simply be dismissed by adult observers as consistent with the sort of overactive imagination typical of most children. It's only when INFJ children are forced to not merely observe the Sensing world but actually engage with it that it becomes clear just how altered their perception of reality is vis-à-vis that of Sensing children. This difference becomes even more obvious once they reach the age at which most children outgrow their fear of trying new things.

• • •

Many of the above qualities contribute to a specific personality profile that many INFJs readily identify with: that of the "Highly Sensitive Person" (or "HSP," for short), defined by Elaine Aron in her book of the same name. HSP traits identified by Aron include a preference for depth (as opposed to breadth) of information processing, being easily overstimulated, experiencing strong emotional reactivity or empathy, and having heightened sensitivity to certain subtleties.

Even though HSPs cannot be strictly linked to any particular personality type, many of their traits are more common among certain types, such as INFJs, than others. Depth of information processing and a propensity for overstimulation, for example, can be associated with both Introversion and Intuition. Additionally, strong emotional reactivity and sensitivity are more prevalent among Feeling types, especially those with Introverted Feeling (Fi). As such, Intuitive Introverts (INs) are more likely than other types to identify as HSPs, and Introverted Intuitive Feelers (INFs) more likely still.

Physiologically, the plight of HSPs can be understood as the possession of a nervous system that is arguably more delicate and excitable in response to stress than the average person's. The autonomic nervous system in particular–whose parasympathetic and sympathetic branches are responsible for levels of adrenaline and acetylcholine during "fight-or-flight" scenarios–plays a key role in stress perception and management. Its job is to evaluate possible stressors in the environment and dose us with the appropriate amounts of adrenaline and acetylcholine, prompting us to act accordingly.

Here's a quick illustration of the autonomic nervous system in action: a stimulant or stressor–someone honking their car horn, say–activates the sympathetic nervous system by providing a burst of adrenaline that brings the sensory alertness required to assess the situation and react accordingly (e.g., hitting the brakes). Then, once the threat has passed, the parasympathetic nervous system kicks in with its trademark chemical, acetylcholine (the "wind down" hormone), bathing our system in relaxation and assuring us that it's safe to resume the task at hand.

For most people, the rise in adrenaline generated by the sympathetic nervous system corresponds to the objective threat posed by the environment, meaning that once the threat of danger has passed adrenaline dissipates fairly quickly. In HSPs however, the rise in adrenaline appears to be greater, sometimes considerably so, than the objective threat; in other words, the sympathetic nervous system response is *exaggerated* in HSPs compared to non-HSPs. As a result, it typically takes longer, often well after the threat of danger has actually passed, for HSPs to recover from an adrenaline "hangover."

One possible explanation for this can be found in research pertaining to autonomic nervous system differences in Introverts and Extraverts. Extraverts have been shown to prefer the sympathetic side, exhibiting higher baseline levels of adrenaline and lower acetylcholine. This suggests that, in many respects, they are primed and ready for threats before they emerge, leading to greater stress tolerance. A higher tolerance means less sensitivity to spikes in adrenaline in moments of crisis. Simply put, Extraverts generally have a more robust sympathetic nervous system which can handle adrenaline shifts in a more systematic, measured way.

Introverts on the other hand, who we've seen are more likely to identify as HSPs, seem to favor the parasympathetic side of the nervous system, exhibiting higher resting levels of acetylcholine and lower levels of adrenaline. As a result of less regular exposure to adrenaline, they can be "twitchy" in response to even relatively small increases in stress, meaning that even if an adrenaline spike is objectively the same as it is for Extraverts, Introverts often experience the stress response more acutely. To use a simple analogy, consider the effects of a shot of tequila on a heavy drinker versus a teetotaler–who's apt to feel its effects more? The teetotaler, obviously.

The same holds true in reverse for Extraverts with respect to acetylcholine sensitivity, interestingly enough. Just as Introverts are easily overwhelmed by too much stress, Extraverts are easily underwhelmed by too *little*. Even a hair too much downtime (i.e., acetylcholine) and Extraverts may begin to display the same anxiousness and agitation that Introverts do in the wake of stress or excitement. Any Introvert who has ever rolled his eyes at Extraverts attempting to engage in low-key activities (a favorite pastime for Introverts) for more than a few minutes before exclaiming, "I'm bored!" knows what I'm talking about.

• • •

What's so bad about being sensitive to surges in adrenaline?–readers may be wondering. I mean, it sounds like a pretty thrilling existence, right? Well, *maybe*... but only up to a point. To understand why, we'll consider the Yerkes-Dodson model, a bell-shaped curve which illustrates the relationship between stress, or arousal, and performance. It's important to realize that "performance," according to the model, isn't strictly limited to action, but can also include perception (i.e., observation and experience). For example, not only taking a test, but also studying for it, would constitute performance under the model.

Here's the basic theory behind the Yerkes-Dodson curve: as our attention and arousal increase to levels beyond boredom, our performance tends to improve as well. And once we've reached the optimal level of arousal, we achieve a peak level of performance–a state where we're both fully engaged in the task and doing it well. This is associated with a positive form of stress known as *eustress* that engenders feelings of enjoyment, purposiveness, and a sense of accomplishment–the sort of experience most of us strive for on a day-to-day basis.

As the model suggests, we rely on some amount of stress to spur us to an optimal level of performance. But this is only effective up to a point: while it's true that some stress is necessary to push us out of boredom and into optimal arousal, excessive stress beyond a certain, critical level causes the curve to slope downward, creating an inverse relationship between arousal and performance and giving the curve its signature bell shape. In short, the right amount of stress can enhance well-being and productivity, whereas too much can trigger overwhelm and ineffectiveness.

Readers interested in testing this theory, if they happen to be coffee drinkers, need only recall a time when they hit that extra cup of morning joe on the assumption that they might need more get-up-and-go that day, only to get more "jolt" than they bargained for an hour later. Caffeine, as coffee drinkers are well aware, stimulates the nervous system much like an external stressor would, giving imbibers a little "push" out of the boredom end of the Yerkes-Dodson curve. The right amount can, and often does, increase alertness and performance; a little too much, however, I'm sure some java-heads can attest, and we become more scattered, sloppy and error-prone.

Human beings are generally hardwired to avoid both boredom (too much acetylcholine) and anxiety (too much adrenaline). The negative feelings associated with these states, such as ennui and depression or anxiety and mania, are meant to prompt us to seek out more or less stress accordingly. Too little stress or arousal is obviously undesirable as it engenders boredom, malaise, and eventually depression; but too much stress is equally undesirable due to its attendant irritability, anxiety and occasionally even panic or mania. The sweet spot then, according to the Yerkes-Dodson model, is somewhere in the middle of the curve, where the level of stress is sufficient to keep us fully engaged, but not so great that it erodes the quality of our performance and overall experience.

Non-HSPs are less apt to feel overwhelmed in stressful situations, moving toward the "distress" end of the curve at a slower clip. For them, the Yerkes-Dodson curve takes a *wider* shape overall. For HSPs however, stressful situations generate a sharp spike in arousal that cannot be contained by the wider curve seen in non-HSPs. In other words, the curve is "condensed" for HSPs–resembling a steep mountain more than a gently sloping hill. This makes it harder for them to maintain optimal arousal since there is simply less "optimal" territory to operate within, meaning that HSPs will likely spend more time in a state of boredom or anxiety than non-HSPs. This may explain why HSPs tend to score higher in Neuroticism and have more episodes of manic-depressive behavior. Does being an HSP sound terribly thrilling now?

This brings us to another important aspect of the Yerkes-Dodson curve, which is that the relative difficulty of a task also changes the basic shape of the curve. More difficult tasks are experienced as more stressful, creating a steeper ascent to the peak. Individuals performing the same task may have markedly different perceptions of its difficulty and will thus experience different levels of stress and arousal.

What makes the same task easy for one person and difficult for another, however, is partly a product of conditioning, or nurture. Repeated exposure to, or experience with, a task generally makes it easier to perform over time. In theory, a student practicing a piano piece many times over will perform it better and more effortlessly than one who has only practiced once or twice. But nature has something to say about the matter too. Differences in personality and ability make it possible, for instance, for a naturally gifted student or what we might call a "genius" to perform better, sometimes vastly better, with considerably less practice.

If we apply this information to what we know about the Yerkes-Dodson curve being condensed for HSPs such that they reach peak stress faster than non-HSPs, the implication is that there's something more difficult about the tasks that result in HSPs being labeled as such; that "something," I wager, is the strong emphasis these tasks place on Extraverted Sensing skills. Since HSPs tend to be Introverts and Intuitives, tasks relying heavily on Extraversion and Sensing are apt to come less naturally and feel more stressful. In truth, HSP's curve might well look flatter and broader if the tasks used to assess whether or not one was an HSP were more amenable to abilities associated with Introversion and Intuition. Indeed, if Extraverted Sensing types were assessed on tasks requiring *those* skills, it's entirely possible that their curves would also appear condensed.

• • •

The foregoing suggests that, to a certain extent, we're all HSPs when it comes to the weaker functions in our function stack. For almost all of us, dealing even a hair too long or intensely with a lower function is liable to push us out of optimal arousal and into distress and exhaustion. And while it's true that performing tasks relying heavily on weaker functions generates more *initial* arousal than tasks involving our stronger functions, it's also more difficult to *sustain* optimal arousal while engaging the lower functions for an extended period of time.

The core issue here—and, indeed, the issue undergirding type theory generally—is one of energy conservation and expenditure. Whether we realize it or not, we're constantly adjusting and readjusting our behavior according to our internal energy barometers. We typically don't like "wasting" energy or operating inefficiently by being either under or over-stimulated. Doing so feels sacrilegious, antithetical to our very nature. And we've been intricately hardwired to detect these energy "inefficiencies" via feelings like boredom, malaise, irritability, and anxiety. One might say, then, that in its most basic conception, happiness is nothing more than a value judgment assessed by the psyche as "energy well-spent."

Arguably, the most prevalent psychological disorders–depression, anxiety, and bipolar disorder–are all iterations of the same problem of energy inefficiency, of experiencing too little or too much stress. And even though we all aim for optimal energy efficiency (e.g., to be in "flow") we don't all reach peak efficiency in the same way. As we've seen, a task that leads to a flow state for one person might well incite boredom or anxiety in another.

Type theory lends some insight regarding the origin of these individual differences. As an INFJ, I find endless amusement observing the interpersonal dynamics resulting from type differences in everyday situations, like when a group of distinctly different personalities is trying to make a decision about what kind of activity to collectively pursue: one person wants to go to a movie, another to shoot hoops, and yet another to sit and talk over coffee–there's a battle being waged over energy almost constantly. Fearing either boredom or burnout, no one wants to have the plug pulled on their metaphorical tankful by engaging in activities they find under or over-stimulating.

Introverts are famously known as energy conservationists. Regularly accused of being "low energy people," they often appear to be storing up energy, like nuts in winter, for some unspecified future emergency. Marti Olsen Laney elaborates on this tendency in her book, *The Introvert Advantage:*

> *(Introverts') physiology is linked to the rest-and-digest (parasympathetic) side of the nervous system, the Throttle-Down System, so every part of our body is attempting to preserve our resources. We are made for contemplation and*

> *hibernation... Because we tend to have less physical energy, we must learn how to fill our tanks with super high octane every now and then. Plus, we must recharge ourselves by conserving our energy. One of the main ways we do this is by quieting outside stimulation and creating downtime.*[12]

From Laney's description, one sees that Introverts lose precious time and energy when engaged in pursuits relying heavily on Extraversion, but an equal or greater cost is arguably incurred in the aftermath of an overstimulating experience–during the recovery phase. INFJs, for example, can't just bounce back into an in-depth project, such as a lengthy writing project, upon returning home from a jam-packed day of shopping and socializing. Depending on just how taxing an activity is, it can take hours, sometimes days even, before Introverts effectively shake off the feeling of disorientation that accompanies an "Extraverted bender."

And it's just about the time that Introverts have finally restored themselves to a baseline level of energy, not even the "super high octane" kind Laney describes that comes after several days of recharging their batteries with internally-guided pursuits, that the world is on them to sacrifice their hard-earned fuel once more. It's not unusual for Introverts to feel like they're fighting a losing battle in this respect. In fact, historically, one of the most common concerns from Personality Junkie readers has been the exasperated cry of Introverts who have reached a critical point where they feel they can no longer keep their head ahead above water, energy wise.

The problem has arguably gotten worse for Introverts over the last few decades thanks to the sheer rapidity with which technology has taken over the pace of modern life. Even though certain advances have helped us save valuable time and energy (anyone for hand washing laundry?), supposedly affording us the freedom to slow down and invest in things that matter to us most, it appears that Extraverts haven't gotten the memo. Rarely content to sit still for long, they've used all this so-called "free time" to justify undertaking an increasing smorgasbord of activities. Though once considered discretionary, many of these undertakings have come to be viewed as essential, or obligatory, effectively upping the task capacity quotient–or "TCQ"–for pretty much everyone, including Introverts.

Although this approach clearly favors Extraverts' preference for quantity over quality, Introverts refusing to get on the TCQ train are nevertheless viewed with suspicion by Extraverts: *I mean, just what are Introverts doing with all that extra free time anyway?* From where Extraverts sit–or bustle around busily, rather–Introverts appear to be doing less with more. This behavior is interpreted as ineptitude, at best, and laziness, at worst. As bad as that sounds (and it is, perhaps, one of the harsher criticisms lobbed at Introverts who refuse to spread themselves thin, energy wise), even worse is the stinging accusation that Introverts are, by nature, selfish. The energy-preserving tactics of Introverts–especially when they come at the expense of acquiescing to Extraverts' requests to participate in their various to-dos and goings-on–tends to strike their accusers as ungenerous and self-serving.

What Extraverts fail to realize, of course, is that not all energy costs are created equal and they may actually get more out of Introverts in the long run by asking less of them in the short run. Indeed, the apparently "selfish" choice upfront may actually prove to be the more altruistic one over time. Afterall, Introverts are *investors* by nature. Like large freight trains, they are veritable storehouses of potential energy: unwieldy, they gain speed only gradually at first, but as they build on their own momentum, they eventually morph into transportation heavyweights, capable of moving massive quantities of goods over great distances.

Extraverts, in contrast, are diversifiers, buzzing and humming with kinetic energy like drones zipping effortlessly from one place to another. Because their feather-light frames preclude them from carrying too much cargo at once, they're required to reload and refuel at regular intervals. In other words, what Extraverts lack in capacity they compensate for with agility: with every stopover they get a recharge. Successful utilization of energy for Extraverts, then, means finding a way to cram as many different destinations into the day as possible, thus explaining the ever-expanding TCQ.

But it's inefficient for a freight train to be encumbered by constant stopovers. Pulling the brakes on a freight train going full speed is costly, energy wise, and Introverts know it. For this reason, ancillary tasks are met with resistance by Introverts who view interruptions as unnecessary detours, frivolous distractions, and a waste of precious energy. Introverts know they tend to perform better when they're allowed to invest in a single destination over the long-haul. As a general rule then, it's preferable for Introverts to keep the TCQ as low as possible, chiefly focusing on whatever they've set themselves to instead of allowing their attention to be divided across a wide-range of tasks. It's one key way that way Introverts–particularly if they happen to be HSPs–ensure they don't fall into the "distress end" of the Yerkes-Dodson curve.

• • •

Endeavoring to undertake too many tasks, especially in a limited amount of time, exemplifies one of two conditions that determine whether an experience is perceived as "overwhelming" to HSPs. These conditions are *quantity* and *quality*. In other words, an experience can be either "quantitatively" or "qualitatively" overwhelming, and, in some cases, both. In the case of the ever-expanding TCQ, the chief object of Introverted HSPs' ire is quantitative overwhelm: the sheer number of tasks is too great to be deemed practicable in their experience.

Alternately, qualitatively overwhelming experiences typically stem from perceived novelty or intensity. A novel experience with low intensity–hearing a new song played softly, for example–has the potential to be overwhelming since more concentration is generally required to process an unfamiliar experience. Likewise, a familiar experience of high intensity–hearing a favorite song played loudly, for example–can also be qualitatively overwhelming since it pushes the threshold of our sense's ability to perceive it. Of course, an experience that is both novel and intense—hearing a new song played loudly—is more overwhelming still.

Such overwhelming experiences are the stuff of which Extraverted Sensors are practically made. INFJs (and other HSPs), however, are generally averse to these experiences which tend to tip them into the distress end of the Yerkes-Dodson curve. In fact, the anxiety response can be so distressing that it conditions INFJs to avoid engaging in *any* activity outside their usual comfort zone. This behavior may actually strike outside observers as a potential indicator of Introverted Sensing (Si). While the confusion is understandable, it's really a misconception as INFJs aren't actively *seeking* Si experiences (as ISJs do), but are rather attempting to *avoid* Se experiences—a subtle, however noteworthy, difference.

Another nuanced way to differentiate between Si and Ni is by how well and how long an Se "intrusion" (such as a loud noise) is tolerated by each type. It's been my experience that Si types pipe up almost immediately when a sensory experience has crossed Si's comfort threshold and wandered into disruptive Se territory. And while ISJs may (and often do) express no uncertain displeasure when this happens, they don't necessarily seem overly "distressed" about it; there's a sense that they have enough control over the Sensing realm to put themselves back into their Si comfort zone by simply leaving the room, for example. Ni types, however, will tend to ignore an Se intrusion for appreciably longer than Si types, sometimes appearing oblivious to it, until suddenly, out of nowhere, they come unglued, prompting others to say things like, "*You only just noticed that?*"

I presume the difference is rooted in INFJ's subconscious awareness that they are somewhat powerless to manage the Sensing realm—the origin of the inferior function problem. Because Si types are already operating within the "Sensing plane," so to speak, should a disturbance to their personal Sensing equilibrium occur, any necessary shift feels fairly straightforward. But Ni types are operating on an altogether different plane: the "Intuitive plane." So in order to make a Sensing adjustment, either in themselves or in the environment, they must jump planes entirely—a move that demands considerably more effort than any Sensing "tweak" that might be required of Si types.

This brings an interesting fact to light regarding the operation of the functions—one that seemingly mimics Newton's first law of physics—which is that a function at rest will likely stay at rest unless compelled by outside forces to do otherwise. So-called "function inertia" appears to be a real and observable phenomenon; ostensibly, any time we're forced to switch gears there's palpable resistance, requiring an extra surge of energy to overcome the inertia and make the move to another function. So moving from Intuition to Sensing, for instance, requires a considerable expenditure of energy that, unless the Sensing perturbation is totally unbearable, INFJs aren't terribly motivated to make.

Echoing the above sentiment, INFJs tend to view themselves as mostly at the mercy of the environment or "Sensing circumstances" when it comes to their physical comfort, safety, and security. In a way, Sensing provisions seem "miraculously" bestowed upon them rather actively attained. Harkening back to ancient worshipers of the gods of earth, rain, fire, etc., INFJs can experience a kind of mystical awe at the universe's decision to bless or curse them with material bounty. As long as the Sensing gods are smiling, all is right in the world; but if the gods happen to be frowning... well, woe to INFJs and those unlucky enough to be in their midst.

Tragically, INFJs caught in unfavorable Sensing circumstances and the paralysis of function inertia may fall into victim mode, expressing their distress in terms of helplessness and frustration. This can be an exasperating experience for friends and family who enter the scene as helpers, only to learn that they're expected to join the INFJ's pity party instead. Attempts to provide well-meaning advice for how to practically navigate the situation are often dismissed by transgressed INFJs who can't see an easy way out. For these INFJs, the Sensing realm brings nothing but chaos and uncertainty, and they remain powerless, should it lash out against them, to do much of anything about it.

Of course, as long as INFJs can manage to avoid the Sensing realm this doesn't present a problem; but that proposition is obviously ridiculous. Sensate reality is inescapable. It impinges on us almost constantly and our survival depends on it. While one could ostensibly go years without ever needing to ponder the nature of the cosmos or the meaning of life, it would be difficult, nay impossible, to go more than a few days without seeking food, water, and shelter. For this reason, childhood is regularly reminisced about by INFJs as a time when life was lived in near utopia, the Intuitive imagination allowed to roam freely, unburdened by practical concerns like where food is coming from or how to keep a roof over one's head.

At this point, readers –especially Sensing types (I'm optimistically assuming there are at least a few of you out there)– might be thinking: *"Ha! Of course INJs like to reminisce about childhood, everyone does. We all would love to avoid responsibilities like having to work a job and pay the bills!"* It's true; there may be some aspects of these responsibilities that are universally unsavory. But I dare say that if Sensing types didn't have something to do–a job to work, a house to maintain, children to rear, etc.–they would be totally asea existentially. Moreover, they almost certainly would not choose to do the sorts of things that Intuitives would as a way of life (e.g., research, writing, doctoral-level coursework, etc.) if given the choice between them and their usual Sensing duties.

Most Sensing types have never stopped "doing" long enough to experience just how uncomfortable, boring, or even downright depressing *not* doing anything is for them in reality. To repeat, there may be some aspects of work they dislike–an overbearing boss, certain types of paperwork, etc.–but they would still rather have *some* concrete tasks to routinely tackle than none at all. In Sensing types' defense, insofar as compulsory work is typically detested more than elective work, even if the work itself is the same (human nature, go figure), it's understandable why they might argue that

Intuitives aren't alone in their desire to shirk Sensing responsibilities.

For Intuitives however, it's not just the compulsory aspect of work that makes it objectionable, rather, it's the nature of Sensing work that requires them to cull energy resources that are harder for them to come by. So while all types may long for the "worry-free" days of childhood, this desire has particular piquancy for Intuitives who find it difficult to keep up with the concrete demands of daily life while simultaneously attempting to meet the call of Intuition. Strictly in terms of survival, it's easier for Sensing types to avoid "Intuitive responsibilities" (if such things can be said to exist–and I believe they can) than it is for Intuitives to avoid Sensing responsibilities. That's a truth to which Intuitives are usually painfully aware, but to which Sensors remain regrettably oblivious.

• • •

It's one of life's little ironies that in order to *obtain* energy, energy must necessarily be expended, creating a bit of a catch-22 for the common hunter. Therefore, living organisms not endowed with the kind of physical strength and prowess that would confer a marked advantage as predators must find some other means of survival. It stands to reason that conserving energy by allowing prey to come to you, in *any* form, however unappetizing, is a considerably better prospect than risking your life by venturing into the wild inadequately armed. This is the oyster bed of reality INFJs find themselves securely anchored to early on.

Ideally, Sensing securities would be readily available to INFJs without necessarily having to mobilize inferior Se, potentially overtaxing energy reserves. In other words, INFJs' preferred relationship to the Sensing world is passive or indirect–much like the oyster's. Having long since attached to the comfort of its bed, it goes against the physiological makeup of an oyster to actively hunt for food. Rather, oysters are dependent on bioflora in the ocean atmosphere for their nourishment by utilizing a process called "filter feeding" to passively sift seawater for phytoplankton at the clip of about a gallon per hour.

To be sure, the life of a bottom-feeder isn't terribly glamorous; but steering clear of the shark-infested waters above means INFJs aren't required to continually expend energy pursuing their next meal while also watching their backs, lest they become supper themselves. It's a wise decision–perhaps the *only* decision–for Intuitives given the futility of trying to keep up with, let alone beat, Sensing types at their own game. Indeed, for INFJs who find themselves in unfamiliar surroundings, it's often unclear whether an object in the environment is predator or prey, harmless kiddie boat or sinking ship. Unable to fully trust their powers of sensory perception, INFJs are apt to feel nervous either way which is why, even from early stages of development, they instinctively avoid straying too far from their proverbial beds.

Viewed this way, INFJs' disposition as HSPs could actually be seen as a stroke of evolutionary genius, though I'm sure several of those afflicted with HSP might beg to differ. Still, it stands to reason that INFJs' apprehension toward the outside world arguably provides a practical edge for their physical survival. Moreover, the security and safe harbor afforded by a stable habitat frees up valuable energy for them to pursue Intuitive aims. In short, by anchoring themselves, oyster-style, to relatively constant Sensing circumstances, INFJs avoid squandering precious time and energy, channeling these resources into long-term (if less pragmatic) endeavors, like producing pearls, instead.

5. PERFORMANCE (n.)

"Get action. Seize the moment. Man was never intended to become an oyster."

Theodore Roosevelt

For Extraverts (and Extraverted Sensing types in particular) there's an innate sense that the world is, in fact, their oyster. Thanks to a natural abundance of curiosity and an unapologetic sense of entitlement, life's bounty is undeniably there for Extraverts' taking–to shuck, slurp, and savor with plunderous zeal. However, as illustrated in the previous chapter, that innate take-action mentality seems to be lacking in more tentative, security-minded Introverts for whom the well-known saying could just as aptly be reversed to read, "the oyster is my world."

Early on, a self-contained approach seems not just preferable but prudent to INFJs who see Extraverts' propensity for action without apparent reflection as risky and reckless. What INFJs fail to realize, however, is that as natural born improvisers Extraverts are more comfortable taking the kind of "leap now, look later" approach that seems foolish to INFJs. Extraverts figure that setbacks and obstacles will always crop up–one can't possibly foresee *all* of them–and when they do, they'll simply "make it work," just like they always have. The fact is, Extraverted Sensing types prefer to try things experientially in order to know what is and isn't working; it's largely by way of "doing" that learning is brought about. For these folks, living life starts with doing something–*anything*–and then making the requisite adjustments along the way. In other words, it's a *process*.

But because INFJs lack the natural instinct for landing on their feet that Extraverts seem to posses, one misstep has the potential to be incredibly costly. To cope with that risk, if they *must* act, INFJs instinctively tend to reach for the most capable tool they have in their toolkit–Ni–to calculate the probable outcome of each scenario. Much like a game of chess, the idea is that by assessing the potential that lies in every hypothetical move, INFJs gain theoretical insight into the best possible course of action, thereby conserving precious Sensing energy that would otherwise be exhausted by a litany of trial-and-error maneuvers.

Indeed, there may be no better analogy that captures how INFJs approach action-taking than the game of chess. Relying on Ni's knack for "if this then that, and if that then this..." thinking, INFJs try to outwit the odds by taking a long-game approach and attempting to stay several steps ahead of the competition at all times. Capitalizing on qualities that contribute to their reputation as seers and psychics, INFJs seemingly use tactics resembling Jedi mind-tricks to anticipate their opponents' next move. In this way, by relying on Ni's powers of perception, INFJs gain a different kind of edge when it comes to taking Sensing action.

Still, for all of their prescience and insight, INFJs can ironically border on naïve when it comes to foreseeing the unexpected–a quirky flaw common among Ni types that we might call "left-field blindness." The problem is that Ni, by its nature, doesn't readily anticipate or allow for outliers and exceptions (qualities better suited to Extraverted Intuition). Indeed, INFJs can get so locked into what they *expect* to happen that they become intractable in their conviction about what "should be" transpiring, stubbornly denying reality even as real-time evidence demands that they revise their original assumptions.

Indeed, little sends INFJs reeling more than watching the improbable fly in the face of their well-considered calculations and predictions. Extraverted Perceivers, by contrast, who are used to taking their speculative lumps and moving on, don't get nearly as unglued in the event of the unlikely. But INFJs without a contingency plan (*why does one need a contingency plan*, INFJs figure, *if you've done your due diligence on the front end?*) are often left feeling defeated and demoralized anytime their usually reliable powers of Ni appear to have failed them.

If INFJs seem incredulous on such occasions, it's not an act. Precisely because they've so carefully weighed and considered their "assumptions" (a misnomer as far as INFJs are concerned), it strikes them as implausible that they might have made a miscalculation along the way prompting disbelief when the unexpected happens. But that's the thing about random and improbable events–like quantum particles, they just don't respond to the broad rules we've come to expect from the more predictable and orderly world of general relativity, say.

At least some of the blame for INFJs' left-field blindness can be attributed to the fact that, in the course of assessing what *could* unfold, they subtly start to shift their focus ever so slightly to what *should* unfold. Almost imperceptibly, as attention is diverted away from simply perceiving possibilities toward overseeing a specific outcome, INFJs are lured into taking the driver's seat and committing to a singular plan of attack, often with laser-like focus and conviction. It's this tendency that has at least partly earned them reputations as master planners and perfectionists.

Utilizing qualities associated with their auxiliary function, INFJs in master planner mode are simply doing what Judging types do best: imposing order on things. While on the surface this might seem like healthy, proactive behavior (*look at that INFJ taking initiative!*), on closer inspection, it's apparent that what's really driving their master-planner tendency is something more compulsory than discretionary, more defensive than offensive, in nature. Such an assertion may seem counterintuitive in light of

Judging's reputation for having a "head on" tackling style, but is supported by Lenore Thomson who argues that "like all Introverts, INFJs respond to a threatened self experience defensively, by using their secondary function to get the outer world under control."[13]

In other words, planning ahead is how INFJs attempt to hedge their bets against the risky business of navigating the Sensing minefield; in the absence of any redeeming Sensing skills, the safest way forward for INFJs would appear to hinge on their powers of Ni perception to assess the situation and then use Judging to streamline that information into some sort of long-range strategy.

• • •

Beyond the fear of being unable to utilize traditional Sensing strengths to land on their feet lies an additional factor regarding INFJs' reluctance to leap into action and go into planning mode instead–one that draws on a deep-felt need to incorporate symbolic significance into the equation somehow. In short, INFJs demand more from their actions than action alone–they must be *meaningful* as well. Action without meaning feels empty and arbitrary, mechanical and mundane: a sacrilegious proposition for a soulless existence and a perceived death sentence to Ni's budding ego.

INFJs love to chide Se types for such action, remarking with not a little smugness how shallow their life experience must be without any "why" behind the "what." Actually, it can be fairly useful to think of the Ni-Se function pair as the "why" and "what" of life experience; but where INFJs get it wrong is in the assumption that the "why" necessarily confers *more* value than the "what." Of course, the tendency for all types, especially in early development, is to assign greater importance to the values of their own dominant function, which is why INFJs tend to project Ni's need for symbolic meaning onto everyone, regardless of type.

Nevertheless, for an action to feel truly authentic to INFJs, it generally needs to be accompanied by the conviction of insight or some sort of higher purpose through which the act becomes sanctified. Doing something "just because," the way Se types seem to, is anathema to the INFJ. Where little or no purpose exists, INFJs will invariably manufacture one to satisfy Ni's demand for symbolic significance. Amusingly, this behavior is readily observed in young INFJ children whose need for meaning is often so compelling that they'll invent elaborate stories–many of which are incredibly fantastical–to explain practically everything, however mundane.

Another way that INFJs may manufacture purpose is by crafting a carefully thought-out action plan or mission statement to serve as a proxy for deeper Ni meaning. Detailing the "whys" and "hows" of intended action with a clear vision scratches the itch for symbolic significance and gives INFJs something "to do" besides actually moving into action, an elaborate form of procrastination. Here again, we find INFJs returning to their wheelhouse as planners and perfectionists, shifting the focus away from concrete Se action toward abstract Ni theory so they can feel comfortable again.

Unfortunately, INFJs accustomed to staying in their comfort zone as a matter of habit find themselves captive to a molluscular prison of their own making. Having renounced Se in favor of Ni, they go all-in on the belief that insight will necessarily lead to action. The problem with this position is that the benefit of full Ni insight is impossible absent some measure of Se experience. In other words, INFJs seeking clarity regarding outer action by turning ever inward for insight are paradoxically cutting off Ni's main source: Extraverted Sensing.

What this does, in effect, is create a kind of closed system that limits the accuracy of Ni's insights because it doesn't allow fresh Sensory input to enter from which to draw relevant conclusions. As I'm fond of saying, "You can't intuit in a bubble." Se experience is the necessary oxygen feeding the flame of Ni insight; without it, INFJs risk suffocating in their own shells. By defensively shutting out Se, INFJs fall into the trap of manufacturing an Intuitive feedback loop that is increasingly disconnected from reality since, without enough real-time experience, Ni has no choice but to become increasingly speculative in nature.

However, speculative intuitions are more the stuff of Ne than Ni. As the dominant or auxiliary function, Ne is genuinely good at sniffing out workable possibilities. Divergent thinkers, Ne types are invigorated by the prospect of adding new hypothetical options to the mix; the idea that some things are unknowable is not necessarily disturbing to them, instead conferring a sense of wonder and intrigue. For Ni types, however, Ne-style speculation ironically opens up a vexing series of never-ending possibilities even as they attempt to make calculated decision about the single best way to forward. Moreover, these speculations are often subject to negative distortion as a result of Ne's subconscious nature for INFJs, creating even more anxiety about making a possible misstep.

Maddeningly, INFJs going down the rabbit hole of Ne conjecture wind up straying further away from the certainty they desperately seek. That's because a future prediction, even if it's based on calculable odds, is never an absolute certainty until it transpires in reality. My sense is that INFJs know this deep down, but they'll be damned before they risk leaving anything to "Se chance." Ni simply can't shake the conviction (desperate hope?) that there must be an ideal course of action trumping all other possibilities–one surefire way of guaranteeing INFJs safe passage through the Sensing landmine. If it isn't entirely apparent what that is, INFJs figure the solution must lie in conducting even more research, analysis, and planning.

Eventually, INFJs find themselves spinning their Intuitive wheels, but never really going anywhere. Thus, where INFJs accuse Se types of being reckless, Se types might fairly accuse INFJs of being *feckless* since, for all their prodigious research and planning, they don't appear to be accomplishing anything meaningful from an action standpoint. Thomson touches on this reality, saying,

> *(INJs) are never satisfied with what they know, and it takes a real effort for them to set limits and make use of the knowledge they already have... the more information INJs acquire about a*

subject, the more it strikes them there is to know before action is possible.[14]

Perhaps this is why INFJs are known to suffer disproportionately from "analysis paralysis"–a term almost certainly coined for them (though all Intuitive types are similarly prone). Defined as *"when the fear of making an error, or foregoing a superior solution, outweighs the realistic expectation or potential value of success in a decision made in a timely manner,"*[15] analysis paralysis tricks INFJs into believing that with just a little more information the path forward will become clearer, somehow making future action easier.

Unfortunately, continuing in this fashion is largely a fool's errand: a prime example of what happens when Ni is allowed to go unrestrained by any sort of Judging. Again, INFJs may be unable to see their way out of the Intuitive echo chamber they've created as long as they're unwilling to put their intuitions to the test with experience. But because they refuse to risk making an error, and because it's virtually impossible to guarantee an outcome with a 100% chance of success, INFJs may feel powerless to act nevertheless.

• • •

If Se types live by the credo, "the best course of action is the one you *take*," Ni types surely believe that "the best course of action is the one you painstakingly analyze for every foreseeable problem and only after equivocating for what feels like eternity reluctantly choose on the basis of it being the seemingly least worst option, knowing all the while that you'll probably come to regret it anyway."

Such is the "shell-ish" nightmare INFJs report feeling trapped in. Helpless to act absent certain insight regarding the outcome, but unable to obtain that insight without the requisite experience; this is how INFJs get caught in a paradox they can't readily see their way out of. Weary of mulling over possible outcomes with no more clarity than when they set out, INFJs tragically find themselves in the exact same place they started: with the dreaded sense that Se uncertainty is unavoidable and that any action they might eventually take is, ultimately, arbitrary.

Dismayed, INFJs will either begrudgingly choose to act in a way that feels inauthentic (i.e., without the conviction of insight) or, more often, they will simply give up on taking action altogether. The tragedy of either position is that it instills–and with each subsequent experience reinforces– the message that INFJs are powerless to exert any real agency over their situation. *INFJs don't act on world,* the thinking goes, *it acts on them.* And the fragile ego suffers in consequence: like a sea-tossed oyster, continually giving way to Se circumstances leaves INFJs with the impression that they have no individual identity apart from the sea–they *are* the sea.

This may sound like transcendentalism, but it really can't be considered enlightenment if INFJs haven't undergone meaningful ego development to begin with. Afterall, in order to transcend the ego, one must *have* an ego to transcend. If the ego is depotentiated too early in development, it effectively stops the individuation process in its tracks. Tragically, by throwing up the metaphorical white flag, conceding a lack of agency to act and returning to their Ni bunkers, INFJs are actually taking a step *backward* in the individuation process.

Such a concession may be acceptable to INFJs in the early stages of ego development, when Ni is just gaining its ascendency and there's little if any desire to claim Se as a paramount feature of their self-concept, but by early mid-life, once the ego has secured more of a foothold in Ni, the disadvantage of an underdeveloped Se becomes harder to ignore. With each bungled attempt at action, the inferior function draws the negative attention and ire of INFJs, resulting in Se being stigmatized as the "troublemaker of the lot."[16]

According to Marie-Louise von Franz in her essay on the inferior function, this personification of the inferior function as the troublemaker or fool is accounted for in various myths and fairy tales:

> *The behavior of the inferior function is wonderfully mirrored in those fairy tales where there is the following structure. A king has three sons. He likes the two elder sons but the youngest is regarded as a fool... Sometimes he is the youngest, sometimes he is a bit idiotic, and sometimes he is a complete fool... But in mythology, as soon as "the fool" appears as the fourth in a group of four people, we have a certain right to assume that he mirrors the general behavior of an inferior function.*[17]

Amusing as this description is, there is a case to be made that, at least from the vantage point of ego consciousness, the inferior function represents something considerably more sinister than a mere court jester. That's because, as the unconscious antagonist to the dominant function, its shenanigans threaten to bring chaos to the kingdom, bringing a kind of high drama to the apparent comedy through antipodal tension. In his insightful book, *Jung's Typology in Perspective*, Angelo Spoto illustrates how the inferior function manages to turn our otherwise orderly world upside down:

> *The overall effect on the conscious personality (ego) is that the inferior function has turned strength into weakness, right into wrong, good into evil, nobility into disgrace, normalcy into insanity, control into chaos, certainty into suspicion, confidence into doubt... tyranniz(ing) the personality until the person wants literally "to crawl out of his own skin..."*[18]

INFJs wishing to avoid being continually at the mercy of "tyrannical" Se circumstances must therefore find a way to overcome their performance anxiety. This exigency is heightened and exacerbated by each inferior function confrontation that ends in INFJs fleeing to their Ni hidey-holes and surrendering the agency to act. That's because, with each confrontation, INFJs have the opportunity to either acquire ego-strength from the unconscious by overcoming it, or surrender ego-strength back to it by folding and running away. By retreating time and again, Spoto argues that "almost imperceptibly, the individual is giving more and more of his or her personality over to the unconscious,"[19] in effect prolonging the tyranny. Eventually, INFJs find themselves compelled to confront the problem lest it overtake them completely.

The origin of this problem can be traced back to the ambiguous point in development when we began differentiating the dominant function in consciousness at the expense of its opposite (the inferior function) in the unconscious: the so-called "original sin." Spoto continues,

> *The inferior function as such becomes a serious therapeutic problem usually after a person has achieved a differentiated psychological type, and in the process has effectively separated or divided his or her own personality into the combative realms of conscious and unconscious life (the good and the bad, the familiar and the strange, the known and the unknown). Such a person sooner or later will have to contend with the feeling of being peculiarly separate or divided from him or herself, a psychological problem that is the modern equivalent of being cast out of the Garden of Eden for the second time.*[20]

Troublesome as it is, differentiation creates the conditions necessary for discovering the existence of the unconscious–a phenomenon that can also be understood as the ego discovering itself *via negativa*. By repeatedly bumping into the limitations of its own perceptions through encounters with what it does *not* know (i.e., by eating "forbidden fruit"), the ego discovers a kind of invisible boundary–or event horizon–between it and the unconscious, engendering feelings of separation and isolation in its newfound singularity. It is, in essence, a recognition of relativity in that "I," the ego, exist by virtue of my relation to something I am *not* a party to which, only moments ago, I didn't know existed at all. In short, it's the budding awareness of "self" and "non-self."

Ironically, taking a bite out of the unconscious brings at once a sense pride or entitlement along with the profound realization of the "inadequacy" of our condition which, though it had always been so, was of no consequence to us in our prior state of ignorance. Although nothing about objective reality (i.e., our "nakedness") has actually changed, by making the unconscious conscious, we have discovered our subjectivity, or our ego limitations, and so can now see what we previously could not: that we aren't nearly as invincible or "god-like" as we thought we were, but are rather like the emperor with no clothes.

Moreover, the fruit of the tree of knowledge once eaten cannot be *un*-eaten, which is to say, once we've been made privy to the missing piece of the puzzle, we can't easily return to a state of ignorance that sees us merely content to be half-way whole. Like a child in his room complacently entertaining himself who, upon glancing out the window at a group of children playing, bursts into tears at the sudden awareness of his having been excluded, the moment our worldview becomes a little larger and we realize what we've been missing, we can't help but feel at once foolish and forlorn.

Having caught a glimpse of what lies on the other side of consciousness, INFJs begin to experience life not as an "experience" at all, but in the abstract: as onlookers and outsiders, much like the child at the window. In what might otherwise be considered depersonalization or derealization disorder were it not explainable by type dynamics, the highly unconscious nature of Se gives INFJs the impression that they're largely detached from the physical world or any experience that would normally be registered by the five senses. In other words, whatever one calls "real life"–and, for the Sensing majority, that's pretty well understood to be events that play out in real time and space–seems to exist for INFJs as a sort of film or movie to which they're merely voyeurs, not actual participants.

The tragedy is that this detachment appears to originate as a result of having repressed Se from consciousness due to the overwhelming intensity these sensations produced in early childhood. For young INFJs, real life feels a bit "*too* real" (see "kiddie-boat-ride-as-death trap" anecdote from Chapter 4), resulting in their confusing fantasy for reality. However, later in the development process, that tendency gets paradoxically turned on its head as INFJs begin to experience reality as though it were a sort of dream or illusion. In what is basically a self-fulfilling prophecy, INFJs experiencing life this way have succeeded in severing their attachment to the outside world by repressing Se in the unconscious.

• • •

It's worth nothing that *all* types feel some level of depersonalization or derealization with respect to the inferior function because of its relative inaccessibility in consciousness which creates a distorting and detaching effect on anything pertaining to it. For example, those who are Thinking dominant types–ITPs and ETJs–may experience significant difficulty identifying and attaching to their feelings. As such, in an emotional state recognizable to others as anger, they may not identify as *feeling* angry at all, instead experiencing the act of losing their temper in a semi-dissociative way, as if it were happening to someone else entirely.

These experiences are what likely prompted Naomi Quenk to retitle her book *Beside Ourselves* in its updated version to *Was That Really Me?* to better capture the third-person way we "experience ourselves experiencing the inferior function," so to speak. Whatever the ego has difficulty attaching itself to function wise is experienced with a distant, dream-like quality–a particularly handy trick for those times when we're confronted by threatening or undesirable circumstances. As a defense mechanism, depersonalization gives the illusion of a meditative, zen-like state of detachment from out negative thoughts, feelings, actions, and experiences (just without all of the, you know, *mindful*ness.)

But the numbing effect created by INFJs cutting off Se from consciousness is not strictly limited to negative or unpleasant sensations: unfortunately, whatever is *good* about the inferior function is also repressed in a sweeping attempt to keep out the "bad"—a tragedy either lost on or of little consequence to ego consciousness in its narrow-minded insistence that Ni be the only game in town. Discriminating between potential threats in a time of crisis simply isn't expedient, the ego reasons, and if a few babies happen to be casualties along with the bathwater, so be it...

For those who think this an unfair portrayal of the ego, Spoto offers the following defense:

> *But can we be so hard on the ego for not wanting to be "burned?" We have seen that from the point of view of one's ego, avoiding the inferior function is a completely reasonable thing to do... Because one's experience with the inferior function is so often negative and disagreeable, an individual naturally finds him or herself in the habit of not trusting the inferior function, of keeping it at arm's length.*[21]

Even still, the myopic ego, whose sole concern has been its own preservation and defense of the dominant function, is no match for the larger unconscious Self which perceives how Ni and Se, as dualities, rely on each other for their mutual existence and enhancement. And while it may be easy to keep the inferior function at arm's length in the face of obviously unpleasant experiences, its siren song becomes harder to ignore whenever we see others enjoying the spoils of its more "illustrious" offerings. Inevitably, feelings of FOMO and envy set in any time we're forced to watch others reap the rewards of our inferior function while we sit on the sidelines.

But as long as our regular, conscious way of operating is working for us, we have little reason to consider the value of taking a journey into the unconscious and its progeny, the inferior function. This is typically how it goes in the first part of life, when we're chiefly focused on developing the dominant and auxiliary functions. A crisis or catalyst, often precipitated by the dominant function's inability to yield the same historic success in securing our well-being, is usually required to initiate a push into our less conscious functions. Spoto puts it this way:

> *Yet because the inferior function is such a key part of the individuation process itself, it simply cannot be left out of consideration without doing harm to the overall personality. There will, in fact, be certain periods in one's life when one can almost be sure of having to confront it: when the superior function in consciousness has reached its zenith, when the individual has become "bored" with himself, when the superior function confronts a problem that it is ill-equipped to solve...*[22]

Only then–in our more trying moments–are we awakened to the redemptive potential of the unconscious which is symbolized by the inferior function.

The thing is, anytime we realize the limitations of our own consciousness, we are suddenly thrust into a spiritual quandary, a place of cognitive dissonance where we're seemingly forced to decide whether to maintain allegiance to the dominant function at the expense of the inferior. For INFJs, every experience that leaves them grappling with how to move into action brings a prickly reminder of the "inadequacy" of their Se condition. Now, instead of antipathy and avoidance, what emerges is a vague and haunting feeling that they're missing something incredibly important by continuing to avoid or reject Se.

With the revelation of the existence of the unconscious, INFJs can't help but fixate on Se–the function holding the key to their wholeness. These stirrings are the earliest entreaties from the larger Self for the re-integration of the unconscious into ego consciousness so that psychospiritual wholeness can be achieved. Marie-Louise von Franz elaborates:

> *(The inferior function) represents the despised part of the personality, the ridiculous and unadapted part, but also that which builds up the connection with the unconscious and therefore holds the secret key to the unconscious totality of the person... a part of the human personality, or even of humanity, which remained behind, and therefore still has the original*

> *wholeness of nature. (It) symbolizes a specific, mainly religious, function.*[23]

In other words, by choosing to address the inferior function problem, considerably more might be gained than simply getting the metaphorical monkey off one's back. A profound and unforeseen opportunity begins to reveal itself: the glimmering possibility that, by reckoning with the inferior function, we might have the chance to be reunified with the larger Self, to discover psychological and spiritual nirvana.

These realizations eventually prompt INFJs to reconsider the worth of the previously undervalued inferior function, kickstarting the first stage of the well-known hero's "journey" or "quest" with the call to action. This newfound desire to bring the inferior function into consciousness is a pivotal point in the individuation process. As Spoto remarks,

> *At such times the unconscious is ready to be taken seriously by consciousness...with each (confrontation), consciousness asks itself, "Do I go down into the unconscious to meet my inferior function...or can I live without these parts of my personality?"*[24]

Refusing to answer the call (i.e., choosing to "live without these parts" of our personality) means the inferior function may continue its tyrannical reign, but is an attractive option nevertheless for INFJs who see the task of confronting it as too daunting; better to spend one's life dodging the *threat* of terrorism, such reasoning goes, than to seemingly guarantee it by willingly diving into the belly of the beast. What might not be quite so obvious is that this path comes with a *hidden* cost in the form of shame and self-loathing–emotions that have the effect of gradually eroding the ego's self-worth over time.

In this way, ego consciousness is put in a seemingly unwinnable position: accept a slow and steady death by continuing to avoid the unconscious, or confront it and risk outright destruction. And though we may attempt to ignore the call initially, the prospect of living in constant fear of being terrorized by the unconscious—along with the crippling weight of shame for refusing to face it—eventually becomes unbearable. Being forced to confront "the devil in the corner," as von Franz calls it, eventually compels us to engage in behavior that she describes as "getting into the hot bath (only to jump) out of it again."[25]

Seeking to regain some traction in the psyche, the clever ego knows it must find a way to face the inferior function and reclaim some dominion over the unconscious. To meet this imperative, Ni types will often dip their toe into Se waters by engaging in what I call, "low-stakes sensory experiments"—activities that make use of faculties routinely employed by Se types in everyday life, but which are instead conducted in highly controlled environments where the actual consequences in the outside world are minimal, if they exist at all. In short, they're *simulations*.

Usually tactile and visual in nature, such simulations can be more or less abstract in nature, but the "real risks" associated with them are always negligible. Common examples of simulations seen in INFJs' Thinking counterparts—INTJs—might include anything from war-based video games (more abstract) to building Legos or erector sets (less abstract). These simulations stand in marked contrast to their high-stakes analogs such as *actually* enlisting in the military or working in construction—occupations commonly favored by Extraverted Sensing types but which have very different implications and heavy real-world consequences associated with their performance.

The obvious appeal of simulations is that they allow Ni types to confront their performance anxiety in a non-threatening environment, allowing them to gradually hone their underdeveloped Sensing skills without all of the messy real-life consequences. Costly mistakes are considerably *less* costly when performed as simulations. And the transient nature of simulations means that Ni types are protected from permanent and irreversible damage in the event that an error *is* made, making simulations something of a win-

win for the ego. In short, simulations promise all the apparent Se rewards with none of the associated risks–an irresistible proposition for INFJs.

Once INFJs catch onto their symbolic appeal, performing simulations takes on an almost addictive quality. As INFJs work to manufacture ideal outcomes into reality, they're motivated to fine-tune their Sensing skills by putting these simulations "on repeat," so to speak. The goal is to achieve ever greater mastery over the task with each additional practice run since every incremental improvement in performance gives INFJs a greater sense of control over Se–the motivation for striving for an even better outcome next time around and a key factor in their hallmark perfectionism.

The thing is, INFJs want to know beyond a shadow of a doubt that everything is well in hand and that Se success will be guaranteed when it matters most. Though they may not be consciously aware of it, by continually engaging in simulations, they are ostensibly preparing themselves for that elusive moment when they can "finally start living." Once complete mastery has been achieved, they reason, they can finally move into action "for real." The result of this ongoing quest for perfection in advance of taking real-life action is that life essentially becomes a giant dress rehearsal for INFJs. Whether or not they'll actually be able to pull the trigger and act when the time comes, however, is anyone's guess...

• • •

I'm reminded of the long summer days I spent with my childhood friends creating and preparing plays that we planned to put on for our parents, families, and neighborhood friends. At my behest, we would practice for weeks on end, running through our lines and choreography over and over, preparing for that ambiguous day when we would finally put on the show for an audience. One morning, at my insistence that we run through yet another grueling rehearsal, it finally dawned on my ESFP friend that day might never come:

"Okay," she said, the impatience apparent in her voice, "but when are we going to do the *actual* performance??"

As much as I hated to admit it, she had a point.

6. PHYSICALITY (n.)

"We are bound to our bodies like an oyster to its shell."

Plato

Readers would be forgiven for thinking they accidentally skipped a chapter having landed here a bit like a spaceship in an old western. This may seem like an odd place to address the topic of physicality given the unresolved tension regarding the inferior function in the preceding chapter which begs the question, what exactly is it doing here? The short answer: that remains something of a mystery, even to the author.

In truth, this chapter and I seemed destined for conflict from the start. Regardless of how I tried to make it fit, to bend to my vision for how the book should unfold, it fought back with equal or greater intensity. Attempting to dress it up and pass it off as integral to the book's flow proved futile–an insult to its integrity and that of INFJ readers. So after a frustrating series of failed attempts, I finally decided to accept this chapter for what it is: a sore thumb sticking out somewhat unapologetically from the company of its neighboring digits, stubbornly demanding the attention overdue it. There would be little room for negotiation. I would simply have to take it on its own terms–however inconvenient, however incongruous. And its terms were, like the annoying jingle of a cell phone during a movie's climax or a zit that pops up on the morning of senior prom, that it make its appearance at the most inopportune moment possible–or what would seem to be anyway.

So goes the tale of how this idiosyncratic chapter on physicality found itself situated, appropriately enough, to the rest of the book, much like the physical body to the INFJ: as something of an anomaly, an awkward aberration with no clear place in the INFJ's self-concept.

It would have been fairly easy to exclude a chapter on physicality altogether. Few, if any, INFJs seem interested in broaching a subject so seemingly banal. More relevant, from the INFJ's perspective, to focus on the more mystical qualities emanating from Ni's metaphysical nature. Indeed, because of the excessive focus on INFJs' otherworldliness, there seems to be an implicit assumption that INFJs are somehow immune to the trappings of the body and its physical limitations–another iteration of the "INFJs as rare" narrative.

To my knowledge, virtually no personality literature addresses the complex relationship INFJs have with their bodily existence–a testament to its largely unconscious nature. As it is, the subject of physicality is often entirely off INFJs' radar. And even if INFJs *are* aware of such a relationship, they may be reluctant to admit it, not wanting to shatter the illusion of perpetual transcendence that gives them credibility as intuitive seers and psychospiritual advisors–afterall, only the "unenlightened" allow themselves to be bogged down by ruminations on their physical well-being!

Deriding almost anything pertaining to the body is a favorite pastime of INFJs who have been known to issue disparaging remarks about those appearing overly fanatical about it. Often eschewing rigorous exercise routines and stringent dietary regimens, INFJs relish acting as if they're above "superficial" concerns like physical appearance. Readers well-acquainted with type theory might recognize this behavior as the vilification of INFJs' 8th function, Introverted Sensing (Si)–the least favored function and anchoring force of their "shadow" personality. Before diving into the specifics of Si, however, let's unpack what's meant by the "shadow."

Type theory posits that the psyche makes room in consciousness for just four functions, including one of each of the following: an Introverted Perceiving function, an Extraverted Judging function, an Introverted Judging function, and an Extraverted Perceiving function (in that order for INFJs, but variable depending on one's type.) This is what we chiefly call the "primary" function stack, or the functions that make up our personality type. For INFJs, the primary function stack is comprised of Ni (1st), Fe (2nd), Ti (3rd), and Se (4th)–the order in which they descend in consciousness.

Yet, there are actually *eight* functions total in Jung's taxonomy: two forms of Introverted Perceiving, Extraverted Judging, Introverted Judging, and Extraverted Perceiving. So if we only have room in consciousness for one of each form, where do the other four functions–the 5th through the 8th–go? These are the functions that make up the shadow–the unconscious part of ourselves often personified as the dark counterpart to our primary, conscious personality (ostensibly, the "Hyde" to our "Jekyll"). For INFJs, the functions comprising the shadow, in descending order of consciousness, are: Ne (5th), Fi (6th), Te (7th), and Si (8th). While all of these functions are, in theory, unconscious, the 5th function is still considered more "accessible" to consciousness than the 6th, the 6th more conscious than 7th, and so forth.

That said, the shadow needn't be strictly limited to the 5th though 8th functions. Technically, any less conscious function could be said to be a part of the shadow personality. As such, during the early stages of psychological development, this can and may include functions typically found lower in the primary function stack such as the 3rd (i.e., tertiary) and 4th (i.e., inferior) functions. Complicating matters, the term "shadow" is often used broadly to incorporate any traits outside our sphere of consciousness–not just the lower functions of our personality type. This is consistent with Jung's conception of the shadow as an archetype representing the hidden side of ourselves, including a variety of unconscious traits of which some are "bad," some "good," and others neutral. He describes the shadow in the following way:

> *The shadow coincides with the 'personal' unconscious... (and) personifies everything that the subject refuses to acknowledge about himself and yet is always thrusting itself upon him directly or indirectly–for instance, inferior traits of character and other incompatible tendencies.*[26]

Essentially, any personality trait left out of ego consciousness–either because it never had a chance to emerge or it emerged but was subsequently repressed–is technically part of the shadow.

But because it encompasses the *whole* of the personal unconscious, not just the undeveloped type functions, the shadow also includes other "negative" attributes such as cowardice, greed, lust and violence, for example–traits we've been taught to repress largely as a result of social conditioning. These "learned" aversions result in such traits being condemned to the depths of the personal unconscious as undesirable and morally reprehensible. However, these negative traits (I prefer to call them "character flaws" for purposes of clarity) should not be confused with the *personality type* traits indicative of our lower (5th through 8th) functions–traits widely considered to be morally neutral (i.e., unable to be judged as "good" or "bad" prima facie)–that we've repressed irrespective of, and sometimes even in direct opposition to, any social or moral conditioning.

Examples of personality type traits, as opposed character flaws, include qualities like being "logical" versus "emotional," "spontaneous" versus "deliberate," and "reflective" versus "outgoing," etc. Anytime an aversion to such traits emerges for which no clear outside influence can be found, there lie telling clues regarding our shadow personality. If you've ever met someone who simply "rubbed you the wrong way" but were unable to explain why exactly, chances are you encountered someone whose primary personality is made up of functions found either partly or entirely in your shadow.

• • •

It's not so much the character flaws we've been socially conditioned to repress as morally repugnant, but the innate, unrealized personality traits represented by our 5th through 8th functions that we are chiefly concerned with for purposes of understanding the shadow as it relates to INFJs and physicality. Still, trying to discern the difference can be tricky: often we cannot distinguish between the contents of the shadow that are innate and those that are learned. In fact, when it comes to the shadow, we often can't distinguish much of anything.

That's because, just as the name implies, whatever lies in shadow tends to be shrouded in an obscuring darkness that makes differentiating its contents–at least from the limited vantage point of consciousness–difficult, if not impossible. The term "shadow," then, is a brilliantly apropos descriptor for a variety of reasons. For one thing, it depends entirely on the object that *casts* it–in this case, ego consciousness–for its existence. It's both a comedy and tragedy of psychological development that we cannot build ego consciousness without simultaneously casting off the "unwanted" opposing content into the unconscious. In other words, for every quality we allow into ego consciousness, its opposite is necessarily rejected into the unconscious shadow. But perhaps the greatest irony of all is just how little say we actually have in this process.

Never is this more obvious than when we attempt to explain what we don't like about someone (as when he or she "just rubs us the wrong way") only to find ourselves at a complete loss. Any line of inquiry as to why they rubbed us the wrong way, even after a few flimsy excuses are clumsily attempted, usually finds its predictable end in the indignant retort, "*I don't know–they just do!*" The fact is, most people simply cannot recall making a deliberate decision to favor certain personality characteristics (usually ones they themselves possess) over others. So, in many ways, even our own ego consciousness remains relatively unconscious to us. Still, if pressed, most people have considerably better success listing the personality traits illuminated by ego consciousness as opposed to those in the shadow.

This same phenomenon is what allows us to be remarkably good at touting our stronger qualities while remaining woefully oblivious to our weaker ones. We typically have a lot to say–often with exacting precision and great pride–about those traits we embrace as positive aspects of our conscious identity, but when it comes to seeing the specific ways we're "lacking," we tend to have more difficulty. As a rule, differentiating the contents of ego consciousness comes more naturally to us than differentiating what lies in the unconscious shadow.

Indeed, in explaining the difference between the conscious and unconscious aspects of the psyche, we often refer to consciousness as "differentiated" and unconsciousness as "undifferentiated"–a concept introduced in Chapter 5. The key to unlocking these seemingly complex terms is in the root word, "different." Namely, that which is conscious is able to be defined and distinguished, named and identified as distinctly "different" or set apart from the general ambiguity of undifferentiated unconsciousness–the formless mass from which all points of consciousness originate.

Although the term sounds pedantic, we all have intuitive and practical experience with differentiation, whether we realize it or not. When asked to identify a flower, for example, the layperson is apt to respond with something generic like, "rose" or–perhaps even more generic still–"flower." A horticulturist, on the other hand, is more likely to answer by naming the specific species, the attributes and features unique to it, along with other pertinent information about its geographical origins and seasonal growth patterns, for example; this is how consciousness works. Our conscious experience, knowledge, and familiarity with a thing make differentiating its attributes, down to specifics, increasingly possible. But where we have little to no knowledge or prior experience, ignorance dominates, meaning that all flowers, however unique, might well be bundled under the generic header, "flowers."

So it is with the shadow: because its contents remain untouched by the light of consciousness, we have no easy way of telling them apart. As a result, everything in the unconscious tends to simply get filed as "miscellaneous" or "unknown." In a way, differentiating the contents of the shadow is a lot like trying to discern objects in a dark room. We might feel around blindly for a while and eventually land on something that sort of *feels* like a vase...or, wait, is it a lamp? Or maybe it's an object that we have no prior experience with whatsoever in order to make a comparison. How can we know? And even if we can determine that the item is in fact a vase, how do we determine what color it is or whether it has any designs?

Of course, this presumes that we have an interest in knowing the contents of the unconscious in the first place. It comes as little surprise that relatively few people care to go poking around in there, as a general rule. Enter ego resistance: that stubborn little tyke on the edge of the diving board, overlooking the deep-end of the swimming pool and fighting with all his might to avoid being pushed in. For most people, the contents of the unconscious, like Pandora's box, are too loaded, too fraught with uncertainty, to make opening them safe or worthwhile.

But why is the unconscious and, in particular, the shadow personality with its supposedly "neutral" functions considered "loaded" at all? One hypothesis is that the character flaws that we've been conditioned to repress have been thrown into the same file drawer in the unconscious, albeit unwittingly, with the technically neutral personality traits of our unrealized shadow functions. The tendency, then, is not for the contents of the shadow to be stored innocently as "miscellaneous" but to be broadly contaminated by the morally repugnant character flaws we've repressed such that the whole of the personal unconscious becomes tainted generally with the sort of callow moralistic judgment that results in its being designated with the crude and pithy label: "bad stuff."

To cull another metaphor, it's as if ego consciousness views the personal unconscious and attendant shadow personality as a kind of storehouse of moral hazardous waste in which everything is infected as a result of having made contact with everything else inside. Therefore, no matter how benign the personality traits in the shadow arguably are, in the undifferentiated heap of the unconscious, they simply cannot avoid being corrupted by the HAZMAT that has come in by way of social moral conditioning–negative content that, as a rule, tends to dominate the personal unconscious. Jung refers to this possibility here:

> *Closer examination of the dark characteristics–that is, the inferiorities constituting the shadow–reveals that they have an emotional (moral) nature...(which) can in large measure be inferred from the contents of the personal unconscious. The only exceptions to this rule are those rather rare cases where the positive qualities of the personality are repressed, and the ego in consequence plays an essentially negative or unfavorable role.*[27]

However, in defending the otherwise benign characteristics of the shadow were it not for social conditioning, Jung observes:

> *But the shadow is merely somewhat inferior, primitive, unadapted, and awkward; not wholly bad. It even contains childish or primitive qualities which would in a way vitalize and embellish human existence, but–convention forbids!*[28]

Still, social conditioning may not be the only factor to blame for loading the shadow personality with its trademark negative content. An alternative hypothesis proposes that the mere fact of the shadow's orientation as a "personality component... with a negative sign"[29] creates the impression of a psychological tug-of-war over conscious energy for which there is a limited supply. In other words, despite the otherwise neutral nature of the shadow, simply being in competition with ego consciousness for energy means the shadow is judged in the negative *ipso facto*. More from Jung:

> *This "inferior" personality (the shadow) is made up of everything that will not fit in with, and adapt to, the laws and regulations of conscious life. It is compounded of "disobedience" and is therefore rejected not on moral grounds only, but also for reasons of expediency.*[30]

Intriguingly, the greatest competition over energy comes not so much from the existence of dichotomous opposites existing as a pair of plus (+) and minus (–) signs, such as those represented by the 1st (i.e., dominant) and 4th (i.e., inferior) functions, but rather from the existence of functions whose fundamental natures are actually too *similar* to be deemed complementary so that the effect of dissonance is more like putting a plus (+) and plus (+) together. This is precisely the case with the INFJ's 1st and 8th functions, Ni and Si.

Unlike Ni and Se, which, despite their differing Intuitive and Sensing styles of perceiving, are actually complementary as a result of their opposite Introverted and Extraverted attitudes, Ni and Si are largely incompatible since both are forms of Introverted Perceiving. While it's certainly possible, if somewhat challenging, to toggle effectively between Introverted Perceiving and Extraverted Perceiving, it's incredibly difficult to alternate between two forms of Introverted Perceiving. In other words, it's Ni and Si's *sameness* that ironically makes them so incompatible from the psyche's perspective.

In the eyes of ego consciousness, there simply isn't room for two Introverted Perceiving functions to co-exist–at least not in their pure forms. For INFJs, Si represents a distraction from and a direct competitor to preferred Ni. It's not expedient, energy wise, to give preference to Si, as energy expended on anything physical or bodily is seen as directly stealing energy from the ideational and theoretical. It is this perceived conflict that is at least partly responsible for our negative valuation of the 8th function, as well as the shadow generally.

• • •

In attempting to discern how the shadow has almost universally come to be viewed in negative terms, we may never be able to say with absolute confidence exactly how much stems from social moral conditioning versus organic type development. One thing is certain however, INFJs possess a personal unconscious and shadow that are heavily tied up with the contents of Si, contents largely symbolized in its most rudimentary conception: *the body*.

As a result of this entanglement, INFJs tend to interpret (and therefore project) sensations arising in the body as dark, nefarious, and untrustworthy–stuff characteristic of the personal unconscious generally. Even ostensibly "pleasurable" bodily sensations like satiety, intoxication and sexual arousal are apt to be met with heightened suspicion and anxiety, as any alteration to the INFJs' default state of bodily detachment tends to arouse negative emotions in the personal unconscious. Naomi Quenk provides an insightful explanation of this relationship between dominant Intuitives and Si in her book, *Beside Ourselves*, and although the following excerpt comes from the section on ENP types, it's also relevant to INJs:

> *When dominant Introverted Sensing types describe the nuances of their internal sensory experiences, one can marvel at the exquisite, evocative images that emerge. When an Extraverted Intuitive in the grip of inferior Introverted Sensing focuses on inner sensations and internal experiences, it often translates into exaggerated concern about physical "symptoms" whose diagnostic meaning is always dire and extreme... Intuitives frequently overinterpret real or imagined bodily sensations as indicative of illness.*[31]

The personal unconscious' entanglement with the body works in the reverse too: anytime the personal unconscious is called into consciousness, it's frequently accompanied by a bodily disturbance of some sort, often pertaining to the central nervous system. This commonly plays out whenever INFJs experience an intensity of emotion reminiscent of Introverted Feeling (Fi). Despite Fe's adroitness with feeling in social settings and interpersonal situations, INFJs can be somewhat impervious to their own deeper and more personal feelings—feelings of a primal nature represented by their shadow Fi function. Should one of these more "primal" emotions (e.g., fear, grief, or anger) be evoked, it's not unusual for INFJs to be stricken with bodily ailments like headaches, stomach cramps, etc.

Complicating and catastrophizing common bodily processes with conjectures about dark subconscious forces seems absurd to Si dominant types (ISJs) when viewed through the pragmatic lens of Si. For them, occasional illnesses and injuries—colds and flus, headaches and stomach aches, broken arms and sprained ankles—are all unavoidable facts of life: things to be patiently weathered and overcome with a calm sense of resolve. While no one enjoys being sick, it's in the face of such "practical" setbacks that ISJs tend to shine since they provide an opportunity to reacquaint themselves with their bodily needs and refine their routines to fortify physical well-being. This is not unlike INFJs utilizing theoretical problems to hone their Ni theories; such problems may be disruptive or challenging at times, but rarely do they seem catastrophic or insurmountable.

When it comes to the body however, INFJs often lack the natural resilience for weathering physical setbacks that ISJs tend to take in stride. Even passing states of mild physical discomfort such as being tired, hungry, or overheated can put INFJs out of sorts and turn them into first-rate grouchy pants. Even when said discomfort comes with some sort of real payoff (weight loss and better health, for example), they may struggle to see the upshot. Asked by my grandfather how she liked being pregnant at a time when many women are aglow with the excitement of expectancy, my INFJ mother could only quip dryly, "*How do you like having the flu?*"

Unfortunately, INFJ's tolerance for bodily discomfort–however worthwhile the reward–just isn't terribly high.

Based on the foregoing, one sees how negative feelings toward the body originate for INFJs, but not necessarily how they manage to persist, even into adulthood. It stands to reason that repeated exposure to various bodily sensations, both painful and pleasurable, might serve to immunize INFJs from their sensitivity to physical disruptions over time. Indeed, for some INFJs it may, as long as they have worked to embrace those bodily sensations into consciousness. But many INFJs have made a habit of simply repressing these sensations back into the unconscious, fueling chronic feelings of distrust and antipathy toward the body.

Sometimes such repression occurs because the feelings awakened by physical sensation in the past–pain, in particular–are so distressing that INFJs have been conditioned to respond with great fear and resistance at even the slightest bodily provocation. This likely begins in infancy, at the impressionable age when virtually all new sensations feel overwhelming. But instead of meeting these sensations with curiosity, INFJs may respond with anxiety and avoidance. This is especially true for those INFJs identifying as Highly Sensitive Persons, as discussed in Chapter 4. In time, the mere expectation of physical discomfort is enough to trigger distress, introducing a pattern of fear or neuroticism that leads INFJs to habitually repress anything pertaining to the body in an effort to protect themselves from the anxiety associated with unwanted physical stress.

This repression largely happens unconsciously as INFJs go about Ni business as usual; being thoroughly immersed in the abstract happenings of their minds means INFJs' chronic bodily detachment is all but inevitable. To the degree that they appear oblivious to the reality of their physical existence in space, INFJs tend to embody (or *dis*-embody, for the clever among you) the absent-minded professor stereotype. In fact, INFJs are usually sufficiently aware of their tendency to detach from their physical existence such that they frequently report their waking life to feel like a perpetual "out-of-body" experience.

• • •

If INFJs' bodily detachment were as innocent as accidentally bumping into furniture or occasionally wearing one's shoes on the wrong feet it would hardly warrant an entire chapter on the subject, however droll. But as we've already seen, the contents of the shadow are rarely all that "innocent." In truth, the same forces that incline INFJs to view their own body as a third-party object or outsider are also responsible for its vilification. As a result, INFJs can be merciless in their subjugation of the body, at times viewing it as something entirely "other" and deserving no more respect than a slave or common servant.

If the above sounds melodramatic, consider the conditions under which many of humanity's moral low points have historically occurred—virtually all of them have roots in separateness and dissociation. Indeed, it's only through profound estrangement from the content of the unconscious that the kind of objectification required to commit egregious moral atrocities, occurs. In this way, via unconscious projection, the 8th function becomes increasingly maligned—a reflection of its association with the "daemon" archetype. Angelo Spoto offers an excellent summary of the 8th function as a moral problem:

> *When a person projects aspects of his or her personality with which the ego is at odds (usually thought of as "bad" aspects of the personality)... then projection may in fact serve to distance the object from the subject. The relationship between subject and object now becomes disdainful, repulsive, and even hateful. The object is so tinged with the negative aspects of the subject's unconscious that we may truly speak of it as the "enemy."*[82]

As a rule, the more unconscious the function, the fiercer the antipathy or antagonism toward it which accounts for the extreme demonization of the 8th function. These feelings may largely exist off our conscious radar until something triggers the 8th function, unleashing a flood of negative emotions. Suddenly, the inner conflict we experience with respect to the shadow is projected outward and manifests in a kind of external drama, giving rise to what we might call an "8th function eruption." (Just to clarify, an eruption of this nature can theoretically occur with any of the lower type functions, but the eruptions tend to be more frequent and intense with the 8th.)

Such an eruption can be triggered by either direct or indirect experience. We'll return to the former in a moment, but in the case of indirect experience, one common way an 8th function (Si) eruption occurs in INFJs is through an encounter with someone who is injured or ailing. Things will often go one of two ways depending on the proven severity of the health malady. Given a serious enough condition with sufficient evidence, INFJs will typically display an emphatic outpouring of sympathy and compassion, often punctuated by moral outrage and a crusade-like conviction regarding the injustice of a universe that would bring acute physical suffering to the undeserving. In this case, the enemy is identified broadly as whatever universal force is responsible for creating a flawed system of bodily functioning, commonly, "God."

If, however, someone's health predicament appears routine, non-life-threatening, or medically unverified, INFJs may become impatient and dismissive, rolling their eyes and accusing others of being hypochondriacs, particularly if the amount of complaining seems overblown relative to the ailment. In cases where others appear almost perpetually unwell and proceed to monopolize conversations by detailing their minor health maladies, INFJs can be especially impatient or judgmental. These illness-obsessed individuals may be perceived as weak, trifling, or self-absorbed in the eyes of the INFJ: *Don't they have anything better to do than constantly complain about a little knee ache??* Here, hostility is focused more directly at the individual as the needless manufacturer of seemingly inconsequential Si problems.

More mature INFJs may be able to subdue an 8th function eruption in these cases by utilizing Ni and Fe to ascertain psychological factors that might be underlying someone's apparent hypochondria, allowing them to show more compassion. They might, for example, note that a friend's chronic backaches started around the same time that her mother passed away–her friend's desire to be consoled subconsciously manifesting as physical pain to create a more "acceptable" way of soliciting empathy from others. The result of this type of insight is a softening of the INFJ's original position that others' complaints are coming from a place of manipulative self-absorption.

In truth, Fe decorum rarely allows INFJs to feel comfortable verbally criticizing others for their physical suffering (whether real or imagined), but INFJ nonetheless experience considerable relief when they discover that they can authentically grant others grace by way of Ni insight. But even if INFJs can manage to offset an 8th function eruption by extending grace to others, there's still the pesky problem of their *own* physicality–or direct Si experience. Ignoring the body during times of good health is easy enough, but at some point there's going to be a breakdown of optimal bodily functioning and, when that happens, any Ni insight or Fe compassion that might have helped temper critical feelings toward *others'* physical problems is remarkably absent toward the INFJ himself. It is against this backdrop of perceived "bodily non-compliance" that INFJs are apt to turn all Simon Legree by subjecting the body to callous condemnation, mistreatment and servitude.

Such a distinction likely seems absurd–even horrifying–to other personality types, like INFPs, because of the intimate mind-body relationship INFPs have as a result of carrying Ne and Si together in the 2nd and 3rd positions of the function stack. Many INFPs make a habit of honoring and engaging their physicality by practicing yoga, hiking in nature, etc. But that inclination is typically lost on INFJs who don't instinctively feel a need to "connect with their bodies" via some sort of ongoing mind-body practice–or any other physical activity for that matter.

Instead, a typical modus operandi for INFJs tasked with overseeing their physicality is outright neglect. Yet despite this inattention to their physical health, INFJs' nevertheless expect the body to perform up to task at all times. Like any slave driver, they maintain the privileged perspective that a basic level of bodily obedience is somehow *owed* to them–a common attitude toward the 8th function generally. As long as it cooperates, INFJs are happy to ignore the needs of the body, even as it labors under increasingly unfavorable conditions.

But anyone can see that this is only tenable for so long. Like anything exposed to the cruel hand of perpetual neglect, deterioration is inevitable: even a robust body gradually shows signs of wear and tear without occasional maintenance. Unfortunately, it's usually only when the situation becomes critical–the breakdown of bodily functioning having reached a point where it can no longer be ignored–that INFJs finally take notice. And when they do, INFJs tend to perceive (or rather project) this bodily behavior much in the way the frustrated parents of an unruly child might: as a deliberate act of disobedience designed to undermine their authority and inflict harm.

At almost no point does it occur to INFJs that the body's "unruly" behavior may actually be the result of neglect and abuse for which they are chiefly responsible. Rather, INFJs often remain resolute in their conviction that any physical problem is nothing but the baseless and contumacious rebelling of an autonomous agent. But as with most things in the unconscious, it rarely dawns on us that we have unwittingly played a role in our projected experience of any problems arising therefrom–problems created, ironically, by our own critical lack of awareness. Regarding that irony, Jung hits the nail on the head:

> *Therefore Intuitives develop all sorts of physical trouble, intestinal disturbances for instance, ulcers of the stomach, or other really grave physical troubles. Because they overleap the body, it reacts against them.*[33]

As usual, it's our own oversight that gets us in trouble.

• • •

On the other end of the physicality spectrum is the tendency for INFJs to *overdo* it by pushing their bodies to unreasonable and unsustainable limits. Sometimes this overdoing is a reaction to a breakdown resulting from the aforementioned neglect, a means of "whipping the body back into compliance" after its failure to function properly. Tragically, this retaliatory approach usually sets off a vicious game of bodily "whack-a-mole" instead, exacerbating, rather than alleviating, the underlying problem.

For example, an INFJ experiencing a headache after unwittingly staring at the computer too long may, in a fit of frustration, take more painkillers than necessary which subsequently produces stomach pain. The stomach pain then causes her to swear off eating for the day creating low blood sugar, thereby worsening the headache and reinforcing the original problem.

At other times, INFJs' propensity to overdo it physically is not so much retaliatory but a byproduct of falling into the grip of inferior Se. For instance, it's not unusual for INFJs to fail to exercise good judgment with respect to their food and beverage intake. INFJs feeling disconnected from the Sensing world after being absorbed in Ni for too long are apt to binge on rich foods in an attempt to "rebalance" the Ni-Se disparity. However, being out of touch with Si–the internal barometer that would help signal satiety–means INFJs overindulge because they fail to recognize the body's need to stop eating until it's too late. The result may be as short-lived as a stomachache, or it may be more chronic, taking the form of weight gain and its attendant complications, such as diabetes or gout.

INFJs may also be drawn, at times, to more patently "athletic" forms of exercise commonly favored by Se types such as skiing, tennis and running. While most would argue that this is healthier than overeating, the propensity to overdo it while riding high on the endorphins of intense physical activity may drive INFJs into dangerous territory where they risk exhaustion or injury from overuse. Oblivious to any apparent constraint on Si, INFJs may inadvertently push their bodies past the breaking point, beyond what types more in tune with their physical limits would reasonably allow.

With each breakdown, INFJs tend to double-down on the conviction that the body is somehow out to get them or to make their life as miserable as possible. Again and again, Si is relegated to the loathsome position of scapegoat, their own physicality resented as an inconvenience to INFJs' otherwise spiritual existence. Convinced that their bodies are somehow victimizing them, they may overlook their role in pushing Se limits and lash out against what they perceive to be an uncooperative body instead.

Ultimately, INFJs unable to resolve their inferior function issues with respect to Se increasingly risk sacrificing their Si bodily health as well. In that sense, INFJs' inferior function problem *is* a physicality problem, lending merit to this chapter's placement here as, tragically, it's often only when a breakdown of bodily Si occurs that INFJs finally wise up to the seriousness of the inferior function problem.

7. TRIBULATION (n.)

"I can't think of anyone I admire who isn't fueled by self-doubt. It's an essential ingredient. It's the grit in the oyster."

Richard Eyre

Before embarking on the detour into the realm of physicality afforded by Chapter 6, we concluded Chapter 5 by introducing the concept of "simulations," explaining their appeal and how they provide INFJs with the opportunity to gain mastery over the inferior function in a low-stakes environment. We cited a few specific examples of how this might present in INTJs, but failed to discuss the larger theme underlying simulations and what it suggests about what is arguably the INFJ's most well-known pastime and favored profession: the arts.

If a simulation is defined as an "imitation of a situation or process" and if, as Aristotle suggested, art imitates life, then one might say that art is the *ultimate* simulation. It should therefore come as no surprise that INFJs tend to be drawn overwhelmingly to the arts in all forms, though perhaps most notably to the visual and performing arts. Jung also recognized this ostensible connection between art and the Ni type:

> *The artist might be regarded as the normal representative of this type, which tends to confine itself to the perceptive character of intuition. As a rule, the Intuitive stops at perception; perception is his main problem, and–in the case of a creative artist–the shaping of his perception.*[34]

A three-part process, creating art involves making concrete observations about the world, sifting those observations through the lens of abstract interpretation, and then manufacturing an approximation of that abstraction back into something concrete. Art plays with the power of perception in that it toggles between objective, experienced reality (Se) and a subjective, conceptual viewpoint (Ni). So when Jung describes perception as INJs' "main problem," he's referring to their deeply felt need to reconcile their subjective conceptual interpretations of an experience (Ni) with their objective sense impressions (Se)–in other words, to bring the dominant and inferior functions into alignment. The reason, then, that art has such a powerful stronghold on INFJs is that, as "idea-made-material," it symbolizes the unification of Ni and Se–a potential solution to INFJs' inferior function problem.

For INFJs accustomed to shunning anything that smacks of materialism, engaging with the arts represents something of a departure from their preference for sensory abstinence. But obviously not all art is created equal with respect to its emphasis on concrete versus conceptual content. Particularly where an opportunity exists to go beyond the "merely sensory"–anytime art attempts to tell a story or convey a message of some kind–INFJs can be enthusiastic interpreters, translating symbolic meaning with the sort of religious zeal one expects from a Rosetta Stone code-cracker. Indeed, this is a realm where INFJs genuinely shine since, as we discussed in Chapter 2, their facility with subtext makes them adept at reading between the lines.

INFJs' interest in the message as much as or more than the media itself suggests they may be more likely than other types (particularly Sensors) to appreciate abstract art in its various conceptions. Insofar as creativity, or what is frequently dubbed "artistic license," is largely a nod to Intuition, the more art deviates from conventional reality, the more INFJs believe there is for them to sink their teeth into. INFJs know that, much like dream analysis (another penchant for which they often have a knack), a story or image needn't conform to "common sense" reality to be rich in meaning. Much of the world's most profound wisdom is found not in the merely banal, but in satirical and absurdist works of art and literature, for example.

Of course, not everything we identify as "art" comes with some sort of heavy political message, trenchant social commentary, or insight into the human condition. Some of the world's most beautiful art–indeed, a great deal–is really that and *only* that: beautiful. And it may take time for INFJs to warm to those Extraverted Sensing experiences we call "art" that they perceive to be largely self-referential (i.e., expressly created to delight the senses). At least initially, it can be difficult for INFJs to overcome the visceral response to Sensing-heavy content as shallow, hedonic, extravagant, or obscene. and they may have to be coaxed into appreciating an experience for reasons beyond "Sensing merit" alone.

Once INFJs begin warming to Se experience however, they learn to rely on their relative sensitivity to the five senses (previously experienced as a "curse") to help discriminate between opposing sensate qualities: the beautiful from the ugly, the elegant from the crude, the delightful from the distasteful, etc. This discovery is a boon to INFJs, as finding an object or experience (Se) upon which to fixate satisfies Ni's need for something to analyze, thus helping them avoid the pitfall of "intuiting in a bubble." Indeed, so-called "high taste" is often a defining feature of INFJs as it speaks to an interest in recognizing when an object or experience (Se) has met its conceptual ideal (Ni).

This quest for the absolute marriage of form and function, object and idea, naturally inclines INFJs to become patrons of the arts where they frequently manifest as one (or more) of the three "C's," as Critics, Curators, and Connoisseurs. In such capacities,

INFJs find the motivation to move further out onto the Se risk curve since one can hardly be considered a respectable critic without a sufficient breadth of experience from which to draw an authoritative opinion. So, it's often, as appreciators of the arts, through gradual exposure to new objects and experiences, that INFJs' typically tentative Se function becomes a little bolder, increasingly willing to take on sensory novelty in search of the elusive "Ni ideal."

But rarely is it sufficient for INFJs to stop at mere appreciation. Indeed, the temptation for to become artists and creators themselves is often too great to resist. To sit on the sidelines and watch others manifest Se greatness means resorting to "onlooker" and "outsider" status–the same detached state that led them to feel dissatisfied to begin with. Moreover, the hypocrisy inherent in the saying, "always a critic, never a creator," isn't lost on INFJs–another reason they may feel insecure about strictly remaining spectators. However, by becoming artists themselves, INFJs have an opportunity to *directly* participate in the creative process–to invoke a clear influence over the Se outcome for once.

• • •

In the Introduction we spoke of the individuation process, the journey that is assimilating the undifferentiated, or unconscious, parts of ourselves into consciousness, as the ultimate aim of all living things. It is this journey, and our faith in its transformational power, that helps imbue our lives with meaning and purpose: the belief that we are not destined to be purely one-sided creatures, but rather to know and experience wholeness, or "God-consciousness," in this life. That opportunity, we explained in Chapter 5, is reflected back to us symbolically in the form of the inferior function which stands as the "gatekeeper" to the unconscious (and therefore our *wholeness*), much as the River Styx to the underworld in Greek mythology.

Anytime we gaze into the sacred realm of the unconscious we are, in effect, coming face-to-face with our own unrealized potential. That unrealized potential (again, symbolized by the inferior function) is an incredibly powerful motivator: it's the proverbial carrot at the end of the stick pulling us ever forward. Would that we could firmly grab a hold of it, we might obtain the surety and control over parts of our lives that have hitherto been just out of reach. As Jung famously quipped, "Until you make the unconscious conscious, it will direct your life and you will call it fate." By pursuing and ultimately mastering the inferior function, we see an opportunity to determine our own destiny–to flip the script on "fate," as it were.

As it is, the power to make art is the power to bring Se things into existence which, for INFJs, is synonymous with conjuring the divine unconscious–an act of playing God, if you will. Creating something out of nothing–a beautiful oil painting, an exquisite five-course meal, a stunning flower arrangement–feels magical to INFJs precisely because their grasp on the Sensing world is normally so tenuous. Putting their hand to low-stakes simulations (like making art) quiets INFJs' nagging fear that they are impotent with respect to material actualization, by creating the comforting illusion that it *is* possible for them to control Se circumstances, if only briefly.

This commonly coincides with the point in life when the dominant function has developed to such an extent that it feels like it has largely exhausted its potential and has no more "room to run" (commonly in early-mid life.) Often experienced as pervasive boredom or malaise, when utilizing the dominant function begins to feel rote and stale we tend to look to the inferior function for fresh inspiration and a much needed jolt of energy, ostensibly to make room for more dominant function growth. Another way to explain this phenomenon as it pertains to INFJs is that their Ni "storehouse" has grown so rife with symbolic imagery that it seeks a new outlet through which to discharge all of that pent-up energy. In other words, potential energy, seemingly bursting at the seams, has reached a point where it demands to be converted into kinetic energy.

Once we catch a glimpse of the transformational powers represented by the inferior function, it's difficult, if not impossible, to avoid becoming completely transfixed by it on a quasi-religious level. To that point, I have said that we can often be more assured of accurately ascertaining someone's personality type based on his or her *inferior* function–the associated traits of which tend to direct our passions and pursuits–as much or more than the dominant function itself. Marie Louis von Franz elaborates on the apparent paradox here:

> *One of the great difficulties in defining one's own or another person's type occurs when people have already reached the stage of being bored with their main function... They very often assure you with absolute sincerity that they belong to the type opposite from what they really are. The Extravert swears that he is deeply Introverted, and vice versa. This comes from the fact that the inferior function subjectively feels itself to be the real (dominant) one, it feels itself the more important, more genuine attitude.*[35]

If the above seems unconvincing, I offer the following argument: to believe that we are driven, as a rule, by the dominant function is to contend that consciousness is a more powerful force by nature than the unconscious–a contention, I wager, more than a few INFJs will have some difficulty getting on board with.

Such is the promise of the inferior function: salvation in the form of untold power over the previously uncontrollable and a meaningful escape hatch from the ennui of one-sided living. Having seen the light, we have little choice but to move in earnest to integrate it. So begins the rather unexpected love affair between INFJs and the arts. Again, von Franz:

> *(Intuitives) become attracted by the idea of stone-cutting or working with clay (in order to) help inferior Sensation come up... for by such means they may get in touch with outer*

purpose or reason, with some kind of concrete material, with matter.[36]

Yet, the idea that we make a "calculated" decision to pursue the inferior function (i.e., that consciousness is in the driver's seat) is a bit delusory–afterall, does the rabbit really choose the carrot or does the carrot choose him? The distinction is admittedly murky. Still, one thing is clear: as long as the carrot continues leading *us* by the nose, we never really have the kind of control over the unconscious that we deceive ourselves into believing is ours. In these cases, the effect is rather one in which the stick and carrot is actually attached to the rabbit such that, should the rabbit actually succeed in catching the object of his desire, it would tragically send him flying over the stick and onto his backside.

Just what do I mean by this, exactly? Let's revisit the topic of simulations. When we initially set out on these low-stakes experiments, it's with the aim of ensuring an optimal outcome (by no means "a given" if left to the universe or chance.) It begins innocently enough with the belief that by controlling outside variables we reduce our exposure to unforeseen problems, putting us firmly in the driver's seat. In other words, by tightly managing the surrounding conditions and reducing the stakes involved, we seemingly guarantee ourselves a "can't fail" opportunity to realize the ideal inferior function experience. What could go wrong?

Indeed, things usually *are* well and good in the early stages of a simulation, when the expected outcome retains all of the idealistic qualities associated with pure, unfettered potential and the eager blush of anticipation and excitement is still upon us. Truly, the quixotic rush experienced here is often so exquisite, so powerful, that it virtually guarantees our continued efforts therein. But then, somewhere along the way, a curious thing happens: as we proceed with the simulation, anticipation and excitement morph into compulsion and frustration as the sought-after ideal slips away, like the elusive carrot, and whatever outcome we thought we had guaranteed for ourselves only results in our fruitlessly (veggielessly?) grasping at air.

There's a particular brand of irony here reserved for dominant Intuitive types which is that, even as they work to concretize their ideas, the hard outcome often proves more elusive than the conceptual ideal. Any INFJ who has ever enthusiastically set out to enact a creative vision only to be disappointed–either acutely or vaguely–by the outcome's lack of resemblance to the original conception can relate. The lamentable experience as relayed by INFJs is that Ni visions, like seeds that flourish in the lush inner landscape of intuition, seem to instantly wither and die once transplanted into the harsh climate of Se reality. Complicating matters, INFJs report that the more they attempt to "work" a creative vision into submission, the more it seems to fight back. What the heck is going on here?

A few things, perhaps. First, because the inferior function is largely unconscious it's almost impossible to accurately conceive or envision in advance of our having actually experienced it. Since we are unable to directly access the inferior function in consciousness, we are forced to rely either on projections from the unconscious or conceptions borrowed from culture in order to understand its nature. But these are approximations at best and, as such, they can never fully capture all of the complexities and vicissitudes of "the real thing." This thorny little problem is at least partly responsible for the inevitable disconnect (and subsequent disappointment) between our expectations and the actual outcome.

The misleading nature of unconscious projections and borrowed conceptions is that they're at once simplified and exaggerated, much like a caricature or cartoon. For example, to an ITP with inferior Extraverted Feeling, true love might be imagined as something reminiscent of a cheesy, 90's-era romantic comedy–a conception "borrowed" from culture. As endearing as these depictions are, most people recognize that real-life relationships are considerably more complicated than these films would have us believe. Similarly, INFJs and INTJs attempting to envision the ideal Sensing life might be struck, simply, by the following symbol: money. Though they may be loath to admit it, many INJs tend to equate "Se wealth" with actual dollars and cents–not the myriad life experiences available to them at little or no financial cost whatsoever.

However naïve, it's entirely natural to fixate on these symbols. Afterall, it's unlikely that we'd even bother with the journey if we didn't have some idea of what we were after. Assuming the unconscious is trying to move us toward integration, it needs to get our attention somehow, and the way it typically does this is by flashing obvious, "can't miss" signs our way like tacky billboards on the side of the highway. That the unconscious is trying to get our attention is not, in and of itself, a bad thing, but problems arise when we become so fixated on finding the literal iteration of these exaggerated symbols that we fail to recognize the real thing when we actually happen upon it.

There's a fantastic scene at the end of the movie, *Indiana Jones and The Last Crusade*, wherein, after arduously seeking out the Holy Grail, Indiana Jones (the protagonist), Walter Donovan (the antagonist, a Nazi) and his accomplice Elsa finally reach the place where the Grail is stored. Guarded by the last of the Knights Templar, the "true" Grail is disguised among a hundred or more counterfeit grails such that one is advised to "choose wisely" before drinking from it, as only the true Grail will confer everlasting life. With that, Elsa scans the display, grabs an ornately gilded chalice, and fills it with water from the nearby fount before offering it to a power-hungry Donovan who, lusting to be the first, eagerly snatches up the cup and drinks.

Now, anyone who's seen the movie will undoubtedly remember the horrifying feat of cinematic special-effects that follows as Donovan's face melts off, grotesquely transforming him from corpse to dust (he chose "poorly"); but the *truly* memorable part, in my opinion, is what happens next as Indiana makes his own attempt at a Grail selection. Bypassing the more obvious offerings, he reaches for a plain, unadorned goblet hidden unassumingly behind a sea of elaborate fakes instead. It probably goes without saying that Indiana chose "wisely," and is therefore rewarded with eternal life.

The message here, echoed by the wisdom found in virtually every religious text the world over, is that being consumed with what we *expect* to find in the way of riches (often that which is flashy and obvious) has an unfortunate way of blinding us to, and consequently robbing us of, the opportunity to discover true and lasting wealth.

• • •

If one of our chief inferior function tribulations comes as a result of being deceived by unrealistic projections and conceptions, another is arguably the result of our being deceived by none other than... *drumroll please* ... *ourselves*. And, conveniently, the first tends to play right into the hands of the second.

There are plenty of times when things don't unfold according to our expectations and yet we're not terribly distressed by the outcome. In these cases, we simply learn from the experience, make adjustments, and move on with little to no drama; but not so with the inferior function. This is readily observed in the course of enacting an inferior function simulation. Despite going to great lengths to reduce as much stress as possible and guarantee a positive outcome, our emotional response to unexpected setbacks in the course of a simulation tends to border on severe.

You see, no matter how supposedly "low stakes" our little experiments are, whenever the inferior function is involved, there's considerably more on the line than we tend to deceive ourselves into thinking is the case. That's because the inferior function, by its very nature, comes with an enormous amount of baggage in the form of symbolic significance. Any failure or shortcoming therein, no matter how small, is usually taken as "proof positive" of our inadequacy in an area that we already feel fairly insecure about, psychologically speaking. Consequently, the outcome of an inferior function simulation is never a wholly separate or objective phenomenon, but is almost always charged with subjective energy projected from the unconscious, often of a "sensitive" nature. In other words, it's *personal.*

Anytime that reality collides with our unmet expectations for inferior function rewards, the result is that we're left feeling like the victims of a bait-and-switch that leaves us flat on our face while the universe laughs at our expense. Adding insult to injury, the more we attempt to control the conditions of a simulation to reduce outside interference, the louder the underlying message that we have no one to blame for our failure but ourselves (but don't think we won't try.) This realization is devastating from the ego's perspective as it has the unfortunate effect of throwing our entire self-worth into question, inciting a defensive reaction in response.

The drama outlined above is affirmed by von Franz, who cites "touchiness and tyranny" as typical aspects of this experience:

> *The inferior function and the sore spot are absolutely connected... Most people, when their inferior function is any way touched upon, become terribly childish: they can't stand the slightest criticism and always feel attacked. Here they are uncertain of themselves... (this) illustrates another general feature of the inferior function, namely a tremendous charge of emotion is generally connected with its processes. As soon as you get into this realm people easily become emotional.*[37]

As it is, the inferior function has a way of putting our vulnerability on display, along with our most sacred hopes and dreams. And that exposure leaves us feeling anxious and defensive when even seemingly inconsequential things don't go our way. Hence, when it comes to the inferior function, there's really no such thing as a "low-stakes" experiment.

I learned this first-hand the year I spent enrolled in culinary school at Le Cordon Bleu's Baking and Patisserie program in my mid-twenties. Four hours into making Hungarian Dobos Torte and the stifling heat from the kitchen's industrial-grade ovens (perpetually on "on") was getting to both me and the buttercream.

Time was clearly not on my side, but I refused to let my vision of pastry perfection be compromised in any way. As I frantically worked to assemble the cake's finicky layers, it was obvious that the thing was getting away from me; it would be the "Leaning Tower of Torte" or nothing at all. Despondent, I threw the spatula on the counter and began crying uncontrollably.

This display naturally drew the attention of the class instructor who hurried to my station to ascertain the problem. Blabbering between exasperated sobs, an incomprehensible tirade of angst and verbal self-abuse regarding the worthlessness of me and the fruits of my labor poured from my mouth into my instructor's unsuspecting ear. Her bewildered expression said it all: the severity of my reaction was not commensurate to reality of the situation, yet here I was in a complete shambles, crying in my cake, apparently unable to convince myself that it wasn't somehow my own flesh and blood into its chocolatey layers.

This is a good place to pause for some observation and analysis: that one should get so bent out of shape over something that, at least from an objective perspective, constitutes relatively small potatoes, is a classic hallmark of what is sometimes referred to as being "in the grip" of the inferior function. To the best of my knowledge, this concept was first coined and used by Naomi Quenk in her book, *Beside Ourselves*, to describe in fairly self-evident terms an experience in which our typical state of consciousness is diminished, allowing our less conscious functions to take control of our thoughts, feelings and behaviors–contrary to what we know to be our usual, equanimous selves.

Also known a "grip experience," being in the grip tends to coincide with periods of stress arising as a result of having spent too much time in the lower functions–particularly the inferior function. Anytime we become overtaxed by a task that demands almost exclusive use our lower functions without the ability to rely on the dominant function to keep us in our zone of competence, we are prone to impatience and irritability resulting from the lack of control we have over the situation. According to Quenk, common characteristics of a grip experience include "tunnel vision, loss of sense of humor, and all-or-nothing beliefs and statements."

Cross-referencing this checklist of characteristics with my culinary school anecdote above, let's see if it meets Quenk's criteria for a grip experience: "Time was clearly not on my side, but I refused to let my vision of pastry perfection be compromised." *Tunnel vision,* ***check.*** "Despondent, I threw the spatula on the counter and began crying uncontrollably." *Loss of sense of humor,* ***check.*** "An incomprehensible tirade of angst and verbal self-abuse regarding the absolute worthlessness of me and the fruits of my labor." *All-or-nothing beliefs and statements,* ***check, and check.*** Ladies and gentlemen, I think we can confidently conclude that what we have here is, indeed, a full-blown, bonafide inferior function eruption.

Mercifully, my tale of cake-making woe doesn't end here, with me mid-meltdown in front of God and everyone else in that classroom tragically forced to bear witness, as what happened next, I'll never forget. Placing her hand firmly on my shoulder, the instructor stooped to meet me at eye level, arresting my run-away rant with her penetrating gaze, and said firmly but gently, "Elaine–it's *just* cake." A more personal riff on the proverb that "there's no use crying over spilt milk," her words, particularly in the way they were conveyed, had the intended effect of breaking the spell. So. Much. Life Wisdom. Packed into four little words. "Elaine–it's *just* cake." That realization seems obvious, yet anyone who's ever been in the throes of a grip experience knows that, in the moment, the obvious is often anything but.

The brilliance of my instructor's words is that they went straight to the heart of the problem where the inferior function is concerned: the trouble is almost always that we've bitten off more than we can chew, practically and psychologically speaking. Maddeningly, the degree to which we potentiate the inferior function by being consumed by our desire for power over it has direct provenance in the extent to which we're ultimately subjugated by it. Like the well-known subject of the Goethe poem, "The Sorcerer's Apprentice," who attempts to use magic powers beyond his skill to direct buckets and mops to do his grunt work before losing control and nearly drowning, nothing can fully prepare us for the enormity of what we unleash whenever we attempt to conjure up the unconscious by way of the inferior function.

To better understand the problem of trying to access the inferior function directly, we turn once more to von Franz:

> *A mistake some people make is that they think they can pull up the inferior function onto the level of the other conscious functions... It is absolutely impossible to pull up–like a fisherman with his rod–the inferior function, and all such attempts as, for instance, speeding it up or educating it to come up at the right moment prove failures... Trying to fish it up would be like trying to bring up the whole collective unconscious, which is something one just cannot do. The fish will be too big for the rod.*[38]

Whatever hope we naively hold for an easy catch when we first cast our line into the waters of the unconscious with the aim of snagging the inferior function is promptly dashed as soon as the exhilaration of the first tug meets the terror of being ferociously pulled out of equilibrium. Indeed, in these cases it would appear that we haven't caught a fish at all–the fish has caught us!

• • •

That we'd managed to get in over our heads in the course of an inferior function eruption ought to be self-evident, however the attendant tunnel vision that goes with a grip experience often precludes us from seeing the forest for the trees. Even as the situation deteriorates in our own hands, our insistence that the event play out as we intended causes us to zero in on what we believe we can actually control as the key to regaining a handle on the whole chaotic affair. Yet, it's precisely this single-minded pursuit of the desired outcome over a smaller and smaller window of control (classic perfectionism) that renders us increasingly powerless in the long run, the irrationality of which is akin to winning one battle at the expense of the war.

And on that note, here's a helpful tip: anytime we catch ourselves compulsively micro-managing someone or something, you can bet the farm that what truly needs managing is ourselves, or at least our expectations. Afterall, if we could trust ourselves to adequately execute a task, for what reason would we waste precious time and effort responding in a way so exceedingly disproportionate to the demand? I believe the psychological term is "overcompensation." A quick gut-check will likely confirm this as whenever we observe someone engaging in obsessive micro-managing behavior, our first thought generally isn't, "Now there's someone who's got everything well in hand." The phrase, "using a sledgehammer to crack a nut," I think, is more typically what comes to mind.

The antidote then, anytime we find ourselves in the sort of downward spiral that a grip experience inspires, would seem to be to take a giant step backward, throwing much needed light and perspective on the demons casting oversized shadows on the walls of our consciousness, or to "cut the inferior function down to size," in other words. But doing this requires a willingness on our part to both let go of and be let go *by* the inferior function. The difficulty here is that although the inferior function is the cause of our agony, it is also the source of our great hope and ecstasy. So, to draw power away from the inferior function, effectively releasing one from "the grip," is almost always easier said than done (though the doing is made much easier with the aid of a trusted friend, advisor, or–in my case–culinary instructor.)

Now, I know what some of you may be thinking: "*This isn't a problem for me. I don't struggle with chronic compulsiveness, perfectionism and dissatisfaction when it comes to Se endeavors, such as making art. I have full control and awareness over myself and the process at all times such that I rarely or never experience anxiety, feelings of powerlessness, or self-doubt along the way."* Well, that may be true. I certainly can't speak to your individual experience. And–like a tree falling in a forest that no one is around to hear–if we don't *experience* a psychological crisis as such, then can it really even be considered a crisis? I'm pretty sure this is the case for many folks as it pertains to the inferior function: no crisis perceived, no problem.

Indeed, if you're an INFJ reading the above paragraph, nodding in agreement that this is true for you–congratulations on being fully self-actualized! You may conclude your reading here, as the remainder of the book will be of little to no use to you. If, however, you're anything like me, or countless other INFJs who have found themselves–to paraphrase von Franz–"knocking their head against the same obstacle only to suffer hell again and again," then, please, read on. Though it may not be the quick fix we've come to expect in today's instant gratification-obsessed culture, it *is* possible to find lasting relief from our recurring headaches where the inferior function is concerned.

I feel I must make it clear that the foregoing is *not* intended as a criticism of INFJs as artists, though it is often interpreted as such. In the past, any attempt to throw cold water on the inferior function has been met with passionate resistance from INFJs who perceive this as an admonishment for having pursued careers in the arts or related fields. That response is understandable, however, I believe, misguided. Concerning the confusion, I likely bear the brunt of responsibility for failing to articulate clearly where INFJs' inferior function problems originate, and it's not with INFJs' instinctive desire to see their Se dreams materialize–either as art or in any other manifestation.

That desire–the one that drives us to want to realize our inferior function aspirations–I wish to earnestly assure readers, is an inherently good one; it provides hope, inspiration, and motivation for a whole life worth living. No one, least of all me, should presume to tell you that that desire is wrong or silly. But, despite the lofty nature of our aspirations, it is nevertheless true that, through no obvious fault of our own, the inferior function regularly gives us as much or more grief than joy in the process of our trying to realize, or integrate, it. However, this is almost entirely the result of faulty *methods*, not intentions.

As I've tried to illustrate throughout this chapter, a direct approach to integration–while effective for functions higher in the stack–has an unfortunate way of backfiring when used to try and tackle the inferior function. The missing piece of the equation thwarting success is our relative lack of self-awareness in the process. That awareness includes a healthy dose of respect for our relationship to the unconscious and its power over us, as well as humility with respect to our blindspots where the inferior function is concerned. Without self-awareness, we allow ourselves to be whipsawed around by the power that is the unconscious in our eagerness to control it. This suggests that our greatest challenge is not so much one of overcoming the inferior function as it is one of overcoming ourselves.

Recall our noble rabbit's ill-fated effort to capture the carrot at the end of the stick. Too often, almost predictably, this is the trap that diving headlong into the inferior function inspires. It's not that our instincts, or what led us to pursue the carrot in the first place, are wrong *per se*–rather, it's how we attempt to go about attaining it that creates a problem. Unfortunately, when it comes to the inferior function, the situation, or set-up, is not straightforward such that we can simply "get by getting." Rather, success in this case requires us to expand our field of awareness *beyond* the object of our desire. As long as we fail to realize that, like the rabbit, we are paradoxically attached to the stick and carrot, then we are doomed to a neverending series of starry-eyed attempts and maddening failures where the inferior function is concerned.

Let me repeat: the desire to realize the inferior function is not, in and of itself, "bad," it's only that our methods frequently prove unproductive at best and detrimental at worst. Still, without any hint of irony, just as we are entitled to our successes, we are all "entitled" to our tribulations, according to Spoto:

> *Because of what the inferior function is capable of opening us up to, we also realize that whatever problems the inferior function may cause us, they are problems that somehow we "deserve," not in the sense of punishment, but rather because we are personally entitled to them; they rightfully belong to us as a constitutive part of our individuality and being-in-the-world.*[39]

From his perspective, to suffer our own tribulations–to really *own* them, in other words–is what transforms mere knowledge into wisdom so that we ourselves may be transformed, spiritually and psychologically. It is not for me, or anyone else, to take that experience away from any individual, no matter how painful it may be to watch someone struggle, as it is only through our tribulations that we discover our full, transcendent potential.

Consider that the human drama and the universal saga we know as the monomyth–or "hero's journey"–is predicated on the *necessity* of struggle, both internal and external, in order to bring significance to the redemption process. Afterall, a hero with no tribulations isn't a hero at all, but merely fortune's recipient, a shell of a man–*nay, a god!*–blithely going about his business without a care in the world. In short, he is an exister. Such a character is unlikely to garner sympathy and championing from his audience; envy, perhaps, but not sympathy. Intuitively, we understand this when we reflect on some of literature and film's most beloved protagonists: all the best heroes struggle not just with external conflict, but with self-overcoming, or internal conflict, as well.

8. ACCEPTANCE (n.)

"I had rather be an oyster than a man, the most stupid and senseless of animals."

George Berkeley

Life is rarely lived easily for anyone–no one should suggest that one particular personality type struggles in significantly greater measure than any other. After all, every one of us is bound to the daunting task of finding and fulfilling our authentic purpose in the world and that's a course that never did run smooth. Few manage to escape the nagging internal whisper of the unconscious which is relentless in its charge to sow self-doubt and prey on our insecurities at every possible turn, and those who can are usually dubbed sociopaths or egomaniacs. *C'est vrai.* The unavoidable reality of the human condition is that we all have our crosses to bear.

Still, for INFJs there exists a set of challenges uniquely destined to befall them alone. The majority of these challenges are actually ancillary struggles that take root from one larger underlying concern: namely, the fear that all of the complex abstractions existing presently with intuition as a formless conceptual mass will fail to bear fruit or be realized in any material way. In other words, that INFJs' potential will never materialize and that all of the knowledge that has been conjured up from the depths of the unconscious will live and die with the INFJ alone, pregnant and unborn—that is the consummate fear.

That fear is compounded considerably thanks to the extreme emphasis on wealth and material success that is perpetually broadcast across Western culture, especially in America. In a society so consumed with outcomes—so unabashedly "results-oriented"—the prevailing message is that all of the potential in the world means nothing without the physical goods to show for it. Unfortunately, the result of this constant emphasis on material success is that INFJs' Achilles heel is almost always on display, making it impossible to ignore any insecurity or self-doubt with respect to how they're falling short on the Extraverted Sensing front—the world is happy to remind them at almost every turn.

What this often comes to is Ni types submitting to an Se way of life (taking a "traditional" career path for the money or subscribing to the "house, spouse, and 2.5 kids" model of living, for example) in order to simply be accepted in society. And although this applies to Ni types generally, I daresay INFJs feel that pressure more acutely than INTJs due to the prominence of Fe in the function stack which leads them to believe that societal acceptance isn't a mere nicety—it's an authentic necessity. The fear is that if INFJs don't find a way to get a handle on their inferior function issues, it will amount not only to a loss of the Se dreams that they hold dear, but also current and future relationships which are equally or more valuable to them in accordance with Fe's place in the function stack.

For INFJs seeking relief from their inferior function problems, it can feel as if there's nowhere to hide. To a certain extent, we're *all* prone to feeling as if our inferior function shortcomings are being "thrown in our face" due to our relative touchiness in this area as explained by von Franz. That's because the nature of introjection is such that anytime we come across someone or something manifesting our inferior function, like the carrot being dangled before us, it's a powerful reminder of what we *don't* have; to the ego, this experience feels like being taunted. Still, INFJs may feel especially tortured by the inferior function due to the seemingly omnipresent nature of Se values that permeate Western culture.

• • •

In previous chapters, we have seen how INFJs are bound, if subconsciously, to play out fantasies that effectuate the vanquishing of this anxiety by regularly manufacturing the conceptual into concrete forms by utilizing simulations–to become creators and artists, in other words. We have also seen how quickly that path devolves into a slippery slope when Se's glittery visage turns on us and transforms into something more sinister than we originally bargained for, its once auspicious promises leaving us empty-handed. By what means, then, can INFJs ever hope to resolve the inferior function problem?

The solution would seem to be found in a return to or reclamation of the dominant function that we largely forsook at the time we began chasing the rainbow that is the inferior function in the hopes of finding a pot of gold at the end. As Quenk says, "A major consequence of being in the grip of the inferior function is a loss of confidence in what is familiar, valued, or taken for granted." Yet, often, it is only through the experience of having "lost" the dominant function in the course of an inferior function eruption that we come to fully appreciate its value as our reliable saving grace–an experience that's like falling in love with the same person for the first time all over again. Quenk explains,

> *Sometimes an intense inferior function experience results in a renewed appreciation for parts of ourselves that we have taken for granted. Familiarity with our strengths may lead us to minimize them, thereby not developing them to their fullest potential...Ultimately becoming aware of an unrecognized or unappreciated aspect of oneself releases energy that is then available for constructive growth.*[40]

Like the character Dorothy from The Wizard of Oz discovering that "there's no place like home," we might never know how much our dominant function really means to us until we've had to struggle to find our way back to it while traversing the unfamiliar terrain that is the unconscious. For the weary and wayward traveler, rediscovering the dominant function is like finding water in a vast desert. However, as Dorothy's character illustrates, what is perhaps most poetic about finding our way back to the dominant function is that the power to do so has been with us all along. Though we may turn our back on it from time to time in an attempt to chase rainbows, like a faithful companion, the dominant function never really leaves us.

What we also find, like Dorothy, is that we've picked up a few friends along the way in the form of knowledge, passion, and courage (Scarecrow, Tin Man, and Lion, respectively) to help us on that journey. Combined, they contribute that all-important ingredient to the recipe for success known as "grit." These are qualities that may have been lacking in earlier attempts to pursue the dominant function, eroded, potentially, by negative beliefs and experiences, or possibly just boredom and fatigue, leaving us with neither the will nor conviction to try for future success. With their help however, we may yet find the strength to fulfill our authentic purpose, to see what we can really accomplish when the dominant function is allowed to remain at the helm.

Still, assuming we *do* find the knowledge, passion and courage to pursue the function stack authentically, from the top down, nothing guarantees that it will be easy. INFJs called to lead with Ni (rather than by "jumping the stack" to Se) will almost certainly find themselves swimming upstream in our culture. The fact is, embracing one's "INFJ-ness" necessarily involves speaking a kind of language not easily translated to the Se masses. Lenore Thomson explains:

> *INJs throughout history have been prophets, poets, and heretics. But in a Sensate culture, whose focus is on immediate*

> *surface stimulation, the INFJ's process of self-discovery inevitably coincides with some of society's blind spots.*[41]

This is a euphemistic way of saying that INFJs should *expect* resistance for authentically leading with Ni. Astutely, Thomson has referred to society's "blind spots" in an apt allusion to the unconscious content that Ni naturally taps into vis-à-vis the more conscious "surface stimulation" experienced by the Sensing majority.

In Chapter 2 we discussed how Ni puts INFJs in direct communion with psychological subtext, as opposed to "plain text." Simply stated, if ego consciousness is the "plain text" of the psyche (the reality that the Sensing majority are engaging with), then the Self and its unconscious content is the "subtext" (the reality that INFJs are usually engaging with.) Ni can't help but put pick up the deeply buried desires and aversions in the unconscious that others may not even be aware of in themselves. It's this "x-ray vision" into the unconscious motivations of others that has largely earned INFJs the reputation for being mind-readers or possessing so-called "psychic" powers.

Jung associates Ni (and therefore INFJs) with the "inherited foundations of the unconscious," which essentially takes thousands of years of accumulated human experience and compresses it into a handful of symbolic, or archetypal, forms and images. That information is uploaded to the psychological "hard drive" of every individual at birth in the form of the collective unconscious, but is more or less accessible in consciousness to those with Ni, such as INFJs, who, it would seem, have been given nearly exclusive access to the operating manual. Jung describes the power of Ni in the following way:

> *Since the unconscious... coexists with us and is constantly undergoing transformations which are inwardly connected with the general run of events, Introverted Intuition, through its perception of these inner processes, can supply certain data which may be of the utmost importance for understanding*

> *what is going on in the world... Its prophetic foresight is explained by its relation to the archetypes, which represent the laws governing the course of all experiencable things.*[42]

Early on, INFJs intuit the duality in all of us, seeing always the "two persons" in one: the conscious ego and the unconscious. However, with Ni's focus on subtext, it is the unconscious that INFJs are primarily reading and responding to in their perceptions and interactions with others. It's not simply that INFJs enjoy engaging with the unconscious side as a matter of preference between two different but equally legitimate parts; rather, Ni bias actually *compels* INFJs to insist that the more authentic or "real" of the two is the unconscious, *not* the conscious ego. From INFJs' perspective, the ego is the greater illusion, a deceptive trickster that, given its way, would impede our ability to commune with the unconscious and experience a higher plane of psychospiritual existence.

Without question, INFJs' primary preoccupation is with the potential that exists in reunifying the ego with the unconscious, which is largely accomplished by bringing what is unconscious forward into ego consciousness. Highly sensitive to inauthenticity (essentially, a disconnect between the conscious ego and the unconscious), any situation that creates psychological tensions or spiritual conflict is considered undesirable. In these events, INFJs see it as their role to play interlocutor, advocating on behalf of the unconscious with the aim of preventing ego consciousness from hijacking the psyche to the point that it's willing to delude itself and others about the nature of reality for its selfsame benefit.

Angelo Spoto speaks to this concern, noting that when ego consciousness "becomes so entangled with projections" (in other words, when it has lost touch with its unconscious origins), "it becomes *itself* distorted or 'false'." He continues,

> *In our modern culture, this means we often act to justify our projections as being "logical," "normal," "right," "rational," etc. all the while refusing to recognize such attributes for what they are: the biases, defenses, and rationalizations of an often unsure*

> *and embattled ego. Projection of this kind amounts to a sophisticated form of narcissistic entitlement.*[43]

Spoto seems to be arguing that when we lose touch with the unconscious to too great an extent, it has a nasty habit of governing our actions in potentially destructive ways. As a counter-measure, INFJs bring the wisdom of the unconscious via an acute awareness of our actions in an attempt to restore balance to the psychological universe which in turn reaps benefits in experiencable reality.

INFJs will usually try to achieve this in one of two ways, depending on what they're up against. They may, in an effort to coax psychospiritual wisdom out of whomever they're engaging with, attempt to sidestep the ego altogether by appealing to the unconscious–a passive approach that favors Fe's preference for interpersonal harmony. However, if this proves unsuccessful, they may respond more aggressively by calling out offenders directly. Particularly where an ego maneuver is accompanied by gross arrogance or smugness, INFJs won't hesitate to come out guns-a-blazin.' And this goes double for ego stunts made at the expense of others. Happily calling "bullsh*t" on those who would let their ego defenses harm the innocent by making false projections about their honest intentions, even the most enlightened INFJs refuse to suffer psychospiritual fools.

• • •

To understand this better, it becomes necessary to discuss the role of the ego in psychological functioning at some length. In its most basic conception, the ego is best thought of as a sort of vessel (inherently neither "good" nor "bad"), with the capacity to contain a wealth of information regarding who we believe ourselves to be as well as how we understand the world around us. A theoretically fluid construct, the ego is constantly building, expanding, and modifying itself as an essential part of healthy psychological development, though it tends to do this with particularly industrious zeal in the first half of life.

Many variables contribute to our expanding ego-construct: our personality type, childhood experiences, physical attributes, cultural influences, natural gifts and talents, education and upbringing, among other things. Over time, a variety of these interests, beliefs and traits are assimilated into the ego as elements of our self-concept or "identity," the fortification of which prompts us to assert our influence on the world. As we go about life, new ideas and experiences continually come into our conscious purview providing the ego with fresh opportunities to either revise or preserve itself by accepting or rejecting such information as part of its identity. Information deemed desirable is, of course, assimilated into consciousness as a part of the ego's identity, while that which the ego finds unacceptable to its self-concept is summarily rejected and banished to the unconscious.

This process of accepting and rejecting information as part of the ego is sometimes referred to as differentiation, so-named because it is the actual process of differentiating ourselves as distinct individuals (individuating) from the aggregate chaos, conscious and unconscious, of the world within and around us. In short, it's the psychological act of identity building. But the unavoidable consequence of assuming contents into the ego is that in so doing we unwittingly create something deemed *worthy* of safeguarding. Indeed, building the ego is essentially the process of continuously seeking out and creating new value attachments. And with value attachments comes fear of loss...

...Enter ego defenses. As stated previously, the ego on its own is neither "good" nor "bad," but is simply a necessary facet of a healthy, functioning psyche. In fact, the ego is arguably a useful construct insofar as it allows us to identify what brings purpose and meaning to our lives, along with our future hopes and dreams. It also prompts us to move forward, to put those dreams and values into motion, to see them realized. Where the ego typically gets a bad rap, however, is in the employment of destructive defenses aimed at protecting itself from perceived threats to its identity / existence, which can indeed produce "bad" and at times even horrifying outcomes.

An ego operating without defenses generally garners little attention since it's merely operating in a happy, healthy, non-intrusive manner. On such occasions we have little need to regard it as worthy of our attention. Only when the ego's defenses pipe up, like a squeaky wheel in need of grease, do we finally sit up and take notice. And, often, it's a cacophonous racket that is incredibly difficult to ignore–especially if the ego becomes destructive by wreaking havoc on our relationships, for example. It is under such circumstances that we are most inclined give the ego our conscious attention, explaining how we've come to refer to it in largely negative terms.

Setting aside the negative traits associated with the ego for a moment, let's return to a more general discussion of the ego as the primary seat of our conscious identity. Anytime we refer to ourselves in the first-person, as "I" or "me," we are chiefly referring to the ego. It's important to underscore the ego as pertaining only to the field of consciousness, *not* that of the unconscious. In Jung's words, "Anyone who has any ego consciousness at all takes it for granted that he knows himself... but the ego knows only its own contents, not the unconscious and *its* contents." As far as most people are concerned, the ego is the supreme, regnant entity–if not the *sole* entity–governing our thoughts and actions. This is incredibly convenient because as a conscious complex, it provides the impression that how we think and behave is largely under our (i.e., ego consciousness') control.

But Jung argues that this is a false perception. Though the ego would have us believe that it is the sole constituent of our psychic universe, in truth, it's only a small part of the whole psyche–a point of consciousness, like an island, which emerges from the larger sea of the Self which contains the whole of the psyche including the personal and collective unconscious. An explanation of the ego vis-à-vis the Self is given by Jung here:

> *The ego stands to the Self as the moved to the mover, or as object to subject, because the determining factors which radiate out from the Self surround the ego on all sides and are therefore supraordinate to it. The Self, like the unconscious, is an a priori existent out of which the ego evolves. It is, so to speak, an unconscious prefiguration of the ego.*[44]

Despite this reality, most of us remain either completely oblivious or fiercely resistant to the Self as the supraordinate force in the psyche. To admit such a reality concedes authority from the ego and, terrifyingly, hands it over to an essentially unknown agent. It's the psychological equivalent of accepting that the earth does not constitute the entirety of the universe but rather is part of a still larger universe which principally governs *it*. (One sees straight away where the historic resistance to certain advances in the physical sciences has come from, as an aside.) Such a thought is often so disturbing to the ego that it would simply prefer to go on denying any attachment to or reliance on the unconscious as a way of life.

The comedy (or tragedy, depending on how you see it) is that the ego doesn't really have the degree of agency it supposes for itself whether it "elects" to cede some of that agency to the unconscious or not. In other words, the authority to divorce itself from the larger Self has never been the ego's to begin with. But that doesn't prevent it from trying when confronted. The ego, with its limited powers of perception, is of the conviction that if such a thing as the Self and its unconscious content does, in fact, exist, it is an entirely separate entity from the ego–not its progenitor and, by extension, *part* of it. Believing the Self to be an outside threat, the ego lashes out against it not realizing that any attempt to quash the Self only results in cutting off its own nose to spite its face.

Yet, however much the ego tries, the greater Self and its unconscious contents won't be denied. One way or another the unconscious finds egress in the form of projections that run the gamut from disquieting dreams to emotional outbursts to chronic anxiety to interpersonal conflicts to addictive behaviors, the list goes on... In more than a few cases these unconscious projections actually manage to overtake our conscious decision-making abilities, often without our awareness that it's happening at all. Over time, the effect is a sense of impending doom, as though we've found ourselves on a rollercoaster with no idea how to get off. From this reality comes the hard fact that denying the existence of the unconscious doesn't give us any more control over it—paradoxically, it gives us *less*.

In yet another twist of irony, even our powerlessness here cannot escape the notice of the subconscious. Denial is simply not a long term solution—it merely delays the inevitable, building excruciating tension and creating psychospiritual suffering until we finally decide to confront, and therefore, resolve, it. The clever subconscious also recognizes that on the other side of the ego's confrontation with the Self, however painful, lies redemption; thus the "lure" is born. Ego consciousness finds itself in the difficult position of being drawn to the unconscious, but resistant to it at the same time. This is the basis for almost all psychological tension, with that which incites repulsion also arousing intrigue.

Very few are brave enough to dive right into an encounter with the unconscious. More commonly, we spend days, weeks, or even *years* flirting with the unconscious before taking the plunge. If the above sounds familiar, it should. Much of what is being discussed here has already been covered in Chapter 5, thanks to the relative overlap between the inferior function and the unconscious. You may recall von Franz's "hot water bath" metaphor; only in this case, instead of INFJs experiencing ambivalence with respect to taking action à la inferior Se, we're referring to the Se majority being reluctant to engage with its collective inferior function, Ni.

Indeed, how many parables have centered on the folly of man's curiosity in unwittingly bringing untold disaster upon himself by opening Pandora's Box, eating forbidden fruit in the Garden of Eden, or staring into the Ark of the Covenant? Moreover, if these tales teach us anything it's that, once done, these actions can rarely, if ever, be undone. Practically every iteration of the "curiosity killed the cat" apothegm under the sun exists, yet we persist in being drawn to unconscious knowledge like moths to a flame in spite of every ostensible warning that doing so comes with catastrophic consequences, the aftermath of which we are often ill-prepared to manage.

At the risk of sounding overly dramatic, peering into the INFJ's inner Intuitive sanctum, Ni, is a lot like this–the common theme being the unwanted chaos brought about by unwisely toying with the contents of the unconscious. Sensing that Ni types are withholding something, but not sure *what* exactly, has the effect on Extraverted Sensors of a wrapped package sitting innocently on the counter; it may draw little more than a fleeting glance at first, but eventually the mere inaccessibility of its contents creates a kind of waxing curiosity, transforming the object from one of mild interest to overwhelming allure. In time, it's only natural for those in the INFJ's orbit to want a peek inside.

But when others attempt to catch a glimpse of the INFJ's inner world, it's often with the assumption that they're simply getting a closer look at the INFJ's *personal* thoughts and feelings. Imagine their surprise then, when upon finally peering inside, what they actually discover is their *own* reflection gazing back at them in a portrait recognizable enough to consciousness to know that it is, in fact, their own likeness that they're seeing, but which is different somehow–a composite image containing distortions of light and shadow projected from the unconscious, rendering the subject simultaneously familiar yet strange, at once sacred and profane which, once seen, cannot be unseen. *What trickery, this?*

Those either brave or fool enough to nevertheless go on prying open the INFJ's shell have essentially agreed to an implicit contract which subjects them to having the content of the unconscious, good and bad, laid bare before them. But thanks to the reflective power of auxiliary Fe, the insights unveiled by Ni pertain chiefly to he who opens it–*not* the INFJ. In this way, INFJs are like the famed magic mirror mythologized in fairytales, interceding between conscious and unconscious realms, revealing truth in riddles to its engager.

One cannot stand before it uttering, "*mirror, mirror...*" and necessarily expect to be delighted by what it reveals.

To be sure, there *is* value to be gleaned from an encounter with the unconscious, but not without requisite sacrifice: the price of a pearl is getting the flesh of the oyster down first. As Jung astutely observes,

> *There is no coming to consciousness without pain... people will do anything, no matter how absurd, in order to avoid facing their own soul. One does not become enlightened by imagining figures of light, but by making the darkness conscious.*[45]

Plenty of books and movies are peppered with reminders that the truth is a notoriously bitter pill to swallow (You want the truth?...*"You can't handle the truth!"*) Still, this doesn't seem to stop others from attempting to procure a taste, if only to spit it out immediately and renounce the cuisine as repugnant—a variant of the axiom, like the song, that, often, after we get what we want, "we don't want what we wanted at all." No wonder Extraverted Sensors have no idea what to make of INFJs most of the time.

Almost no one opens the INFJ's shell expecting to come face-to-face with their own unconscious shadow which contains all of the uncomfortable truths about ourselves that, as a rule, we'd prefer keep safely locked away. In light of this fact, many INFJs simply opt to shutter Ni from the view of family and friends in a noble, if not presumptuous, attempt to shield loved ones from exposing themselves to unwanted suffering. This can be a source of incredible turmoil for INFJs who, as the chosen translators of Ni, often feel doomed as ill-fated messengers, caught between Ni's demand for truth through insight and Fe's desire to appease people.

The rather tragic irony of the Ni-Fe combo is that it provides INFJs with the ability to reveal others' unconscious thoughts and feelings, but then frustratingly bars them from doing so as a result of same and the awareness that such revelations aren't likely to be well-received. INFJs intuiting their audience will be unable to receive insight without great psychological resistance or interpersonal disharmony often feel the uncomfortable pangs of cognitive dissonance as they try to decide whether to give Ni its voice despite Fe's protests. It comes as no surprise then that INFJs are not easily coaxed into opening their shells to let spill the contents of Intuition on demand–a far too reckless and risky maneuver.

Instead, INFJs prefer to test the receptivity of others' palates by hinting ever so subtly at Intuition's contents with a sort of allusory amuse-bouche. Depending on how well that goes down, INFJs may or may not feel comfortable divulging more candid information about the theories they're working. Frequently, however, the benefit of a preview isn't even afforded to potential epicures; INFJs, with their adroit people-reading skills, tend to be keenly aware of how digestible Intuition's contents are likely to be prior to ever actually offering a taste. They know that serving even a scrap of Ni's exotic fare to obviously unadventurous palates would be an exercise in futility–a waste of their precious handiwork. *No point casting pearls before swine*, INFJs figure.

• • •

I often wonder that the primary reason INFJs cling so steadfastly to the "rare" distinction is to ameliorate by euphemism the profound loneliness that accompanies feeling so incredibly misunderstood at times; afterall, being "rare" goes down the gullet of self-conceit more easily than being "lonely" does. Any INFJ who has ever attempted to explain an insight into one of the more obscure aspects of the unconscious side of the human experience only to be met with the exasperated look of someone who may as well have just been told, "*I see dead people,*" knows exactly what I'm talking about.

In short, Introverted Intuitives represent the collective unconscious to the Se majority's ego. Yet, the foregoing makes evident that any entanglement with the unconscious represents nothing but strife and suffering to an otherwise quiet ego existence.

Being forced to confront the unconscious seemingly puts the ego in an unwinnable paradox: surrender and accept the pain that comes with the death of the ego, or wage war against it only to get sacrificed in battle. Wishing to avert an apparent Catch-22, the ego, with its clever instinct for survival, usually takes a path of avoidance by simply ignoring or denying the reality of the unconscious whenever possible. This is what INFJs attempting to bring Ni knowledge forward into consciousness are up against on a society-wide scale.

Of this quandary, there is perhaps no description both as pointed and poignant as the first-person account offered by Jung himself, who described his own experience as an Intuitive Introvert thusly,

> *As a child I felt myself to be alone, and I am still, because I know things and must hint at things which others apparently know nothing of, and for the most part do not want to know. Loneliness does not come from having no people about one, but from being unable to communicate things that seem important to oneself, or from holding certain views which others find inadmissible.*[46]

From Jung's description, it's understandable why INFJs may feel compelled to bypass Ni and move straight to Se in order to manifest some semblance of normalcy and acceptance in society. But, for those INFJs who have already suffered their inferior function tribulations, the appeal of this approach has largely lost its luster. Realizing that there is no such thing as a "shortcut" to actualization means INFJs find it easier to embrace, or *accept*, their authentic calling–a calling that prioritizes Ni ahead of Se in accordance with the function stack.

Acceptance in this case is really a two-part process. The first, often realized in the aftermath of an inferior function crisis, involves coming to terms with what cannot be easily changed about the world and others. As we discussed at the end of Chapter 7, that means letting go of unrealistic, often perfectionistic, standards and expectations with respect to material outcomes–and that includes how *others* go about the process of self-actualizing. It's simply unrealistic for INFJs to expect Se types to possess the sort of insight or awareness into the unconscious that Ni regularly affords them; such strength of Intuition would require an impressive level of personal growth and self-awareness from Sensing types that is, frankly, unfair to ask of them.

Second, it requires INFJs to come to a place of *self*-acceptance, appreciating the role they are being asked to play in the universe without irony or a sense of victimhood. Tragically, I have seen a number of INFJs who allow feeling misunderstood to justify a cynical and misanthropic worldview over their perceived status as "outcasts," sabotaging an otherwise promising future in which they might generate some meaningful change in the world or, if nothing else, find a shred of personal happiness for themselves. My fervent plea is that INFJs resist the temptation to feel victimized by their scarcity as it tends to have an immobilizing effect which impedes development–yet another reason I encourage INFJs to shy away from constantly referencing their "rare" status.

As it is, the unavoidable price of authenticity for INFJs is regularly feeling misunderstood and experiencing occasional bouts of loneliness as a result of the pervasive Se values in our culture that tend to elide the unconscious wisdom of Ni. The sooner INFJs accept that reality, do their grieving, and move on, the sooner they can get on with the important business of actualizing. Many INFJs have successfully made the transition by seeing this as more of a challenge than a curse–a call to rise to the occasion as the need for knowledge that looks inward into the unconscious is arguably greatest at precisely those moments when the collective ethos has overwhelmingly concluded that conscious, outward experience is all that really matters.

It might also be argued that INFJs have actually been given a blessing in disguise not readily available to Se types: the relative likelihood of achieving self-actualization as a *result of* their being in the minority. As noted earlier, INFJs do not have the luxury of remaining impervious to their blindspots for very long given our Se-heavy culture. But being forced to grapple young and early with the inferior function means that INFJs get a relative "push" out of the nest ahead of other types when it comes to the individuation process. That's because having to face the inferior function forces us to look inward and wrestle with our personal demons, humbling the ego and making space for the unconscious to enter as a result–an important catalyst for self-growth.

However, for Extraverted Sensors, whose primary mode of operating is continually being upheld and validated by popular culture, there is less, incentive wise, forcing them to contend with the inferior function in any meaningful way. While this makes realizing the upper half of the function stack easier for them, it provides relatively little impetus to work on developing the lower half of the stack because, well, *if it ain't broke...* But one can't fully self-actualize without finding a way to integrate the *entire* function stack, meaning many Sensors will stall out about halfway through the individuation process. This can leave them tripping over the inferior function and grappling with questions of meaning and spirituality late in life relative to Intuitive types who have been forced to wrestle with these issues early on.

9. ACTUALIZATION (n.)

"All art is autobiographical. The pearl is the oyster's autobiography."

Federico Fellini

Whether we realize it or not, a key psychological force driving our actions is the desire–or expectation, even–that we receive some sort of reward or "payout" in the form of the inferior function for services rendered by the functions higher in the stack. Indeed, the promise of inferior function rewards is a large part of what compels us to put the dominant function to work so that we might actualize. The ability to earn the spoils of the inferior function by utilizing functions higher in the stack is such an integral part of the actualization equation that, should the reward pathway be blocked in some way, the result is often frustration, resentment, shame or anxiety with respect to our self-worth.

For INFJs this means finding a way to translate Ni insight into something of concrete Se value. A significant part of this challenge, however, is that the utility of what INFJs have to offer by way of Ni is not readily recognized or appreciated by the Se majority. An ISTP craftsman who builds furniture for a living shouldn't have too much difficulty putting a price tag on a coffee table, for example; but just what, exactly, is the value of insight that translates to a deeper understanding of unconscious knowledge so that we might fully realize our potential? That's considerably harder to quantify. Jung acknowledges this quandary saying:

> *From an Extraverted and rationalistic standpoint, these types (INFJs) are indeed the most useless of men. But, viewed from a higher standpoint, they are living evidence that this rich and varied world with its overflowing and intoxicating life is not purely external, but also exists within...*[47]

Unfortunately, INFJs hoping that those with Se sensibilities are suddenly going to recognize the value of seeing things from their "higher standpoint" are in for a long wait. Though it would certainly make the actualization process easier, INFJs cannot expect Se types to automatically grasp the worth of what Ni has to offer; afterall, if they could, then they wouldn't actually be Se types, they'd be Introverted Intuitives! It therefore falls on *INFJs* to find a way to bring forth this rich inner experience that Jung describes and convey it outwardly to the Se masses. As it's often said, "If the mountain won't come to Muhammad..."

• • •

One way that INFJs attempt to convey the value of their intuitive visions and insights, as we already know, is via the creation of tangible forms such as art; however, if or when that fails (either because the Sensing majority cannot grasp the significance of what INFJs have created, or because INFJs lack the technical skills to effectively manufacture their vision into reality, INFJs will once again turn to the power of language to try and translate their normally ineffable internal experiences into expressible phrases.

But this, too, is not an easy task. At first blush, the language of Ni appears fanciful and arcane, largely incomprehensible due to its relative contextlessness, which results in INFJs coming across as crazies and kooks. Jung elaborates:

> *The peculiar nature of Introverted Intuition, if it gains the ascendency, produces a peculiar type of man: the mystical dreamer and seer on the one hand, the artist and crank on the other...*[48]

Regarding the "crank," he continues,

> *His language is not the one currently spoken–it has become too subjective. His arguments lack the convincing power of reason. He can only profess or proclaim. His is "the voice of one crying in the wilderness.*[49]

Not surprisingly, INFJs (as well as INTJs) often report feeling ill-fated to be as Cassandra of Greek mythology: destined to know and profess truth, but never to be believed. In fact, it's not at all uncommon for INFJs to experience recurring dreams in which they go to speak at critical moments only to discover that they've been rendered mute, unable to make any words come out. Despite having what they believe to be valuable knowledge that could forestall impending disaster, preventing unnecessary harm and suffering, INFJs who are unable to effectively communicate the practical urgency of such information are unlikely to be taken seriously by the Sensing community writ large.

Afterall, the only difference between a crank and a genius is the ability to articulate clearly the pathway of reasoning that has led to his or her conclusions, *and*–it's worth noting–to the point that others actually find it believable. Many unfortunate INFJs who came before and failed to effectively convince others have ultimately suffered the fate typical of witches and heretics. I have to believe that those hangings, burnings and crucifixions are somehow inked indelibly on the collective unconscious and that anxious INFJs everywhere still live with the shadowy fear that they could be perceived as dissidents or lunatics at any time and swiftly put to an end. For that reason alone, many INFJs have concluded that when it comes to communicating the abstrusities of Ni, as a rule, it's better to simply keep one's mouth shut.

Another problem with respect to communication is that INFJs can be so stubbornly convinced of the "self-evident" nature of their intuitive insights that they refuse to clarify or elaborate on them for fear that they'll get watered down in the process. Using too direct or simple terms can feel like "selling-out" to INFJs–the result being a cheapening effect on what they're attempting to convey. After going to great lengths to explain what they consider to be a profound insight, among the INFJs' greatest scourges is being met with the casual rejoinder, "*Is that all?*" Like a magician mastering the art of illusion, for INFJs there always exists the thorny problem of revealing enough of the unconscious so as to effectively captivate one's audience, but not so much that he risks giving away the trick and so breaks the spell.

It's a fine line to walk: INFJs know that a considerable amount of Ni's allure is owed to its obscurity, but unfortunately so is its failure to be noticed, appreciated and understood. Afterall, would you pay to see a magician perform a trick if you knew how it was done? What about paying to see a trick *not* be performed? Unlikely. As with any successful illusion, pay dirt in this case lies in being convincing, but not *too* convincing. And INFJs know audiences have a way of being fickle. They often clamor one moment only to crucify the next, adding to the pressure INFJs feel to perform perfectly, otherwise not performing at all. As Lenore Thomson notes,

> *(INJs') unconscious Sensate impulses fill them with a yearning for credit and recognition, but they may be increasingly critical of their opportunities to make a contribution or so dissatisfied with their efforts that they don't share them with others.*[50]

But this would be a critical mistake. To throw in the towel on trying to communicate Ni's insights is to effectively cut the actualization process off at the knees for INFJs–a costly error, spiritually. Though it's a real possibility that INFJs' insights won't be appreciated if they're shared, it's an absolute *certainty* that they won't be if they're not. Common sense says the odds of actualizing favor the former.

INFJs being honest with themselves will further recognize that by presuming to know the outcome of their efforts in advance of having actually *made* the effort, and subsequently using that presumption to dictate their actions (or lack of action, in this case), they are impeding the same unconscious forces they profess to promote and defend as a core tenet of their belief system. Afterall, how can INFJs expect Sensing types to take a leap of faith when it comes to being open to the miracles afforded by unconscious Intuition if they can't make the same effort where unconscious Sensing is concerned? INFJs are, in effect, trying to preemptively control something that they never had–nor ever will have–much, if any, control over: how their insights will actually land once they're in the hands (or ears, rather) of Sensing types.

In truth, such attempts on the part of INFJs are little more than dressed-up grip behaviors masquerading as action taken authentically at the behest of Intuition in the form of "psychic foresight"–a passive-aggressive attempt to control the inferior function by wielding the dominant function like a kind of weapon or bargaining tool. INFJs who do this appear to be giving the unconscious an ultimatum of sorts, threatening to hold their Ni insights hostage unless or until Se circumstances prove worthy to receive them. *What arrogance!* And yet it's understandable since what we do from a place of pride, we ultimately do from a place of fear. In this case, it's the fear that if we dare to sacrifice something of value from the dominant function, the universe won't hold up its end of the bargain and give us the inferior function rewards we were desperately counting on in return. (Remember that bit in the first paragraph about our expectation of an inferior function "payout"?)

One sees straight away where the problem lies and it's in that nerve-wracking moment of uncertainty between releasing the hostage (Ni) and getting our hands on the loot (Se), otherwise known as "the exchange." A classic prisoner's dilemma, mutual satisfaction in this case paradoxically requires trust to emerge from a place fraught with uncertainty. The absurdity of such situations is captured with not a little humor in those movies where the parties square off at a distance, clutching their valuables while inching tentatively toward one another shouting, "*You go first!*"... "*No, YOU go first!*" Desperate to escape the tension arising from the possibility of a zero-sum outcome, the anxious viewer finds himself cheering for a leap of faith on the part of one or both parties knowing that, without one, we'd never get from "the standoff" to "the handoff." The fundamental need for trust, in other words, is baked into the cake.

As it happens, I can't think of a single, major religion that advocates taking a "you go first" approach to acts of faith in our interactions with God and others as the key to our spiritual salubrity. Ironically, what we in our avarice consistently fail to recognize is that our lack of faith in the other party (i.e., the unconscious) to deliver is really a lack of faith in the relative "valuelessness" of what we're holding in consciousness as collateral. What do I mean by that, exactly? I mean, we tend to put far too high a premium on the value of our own dominant function, the implication of which–and here's the kicker–is that we ultimately lack the confidence in *ourselves* to get or produce more of our own "essence" if need be. But when we have faith in the abundance of our dominant function, there's little or no need for parsimony in an exchange. Indeed, it's surprising just how easy it is to "go first" when you believe there's always more where that came from.

• • •

Once INFJs realize that the font of Ni springs eternal–typically in the aftermath of an inferior function tribulation–there is considerably less inclining them to be stingy or withholding where their intuitive insights are concerned. That's the beauty of having experienced a confrontation with the unconscious and making it to the other side: it generates renewed confidence, appreciation and enthusiasm for the bounty of what is provided to us in consciousness by way of the dominant function. And because INFJs have well and truly learned that producing intuitive insights is intrinsically satisfying on its own (irrespective of Se outcomes, in other words) there is considerably less room for a scarcity mindset—the gateway for all grip experiences—to enter.

But the journey to actualization does not and *cannot* end with INFJs simply pledging (or re-pledging) allegiance to the dominant function in consciousness; this is only the first, however necessary, step. There still remains the pesky problem of translating the value of intuitive knowledge into something recognizable to the masses. When it comes to that task, many INFJs up to this point have focused almost exclusively on the "problem of perception," as Jung calls it, bouncing between their Ni visions and Se experience with the primary aim being descriptive in nature. As we've seen however, this descriptive approach—along, perhaps, with Fe thrown in which serves as a vehicle for evangelizing Ni's insights—tends to have the opposite intended effect by producing the "crank-like appearance" that Jung described earlier and ultimately alienating others instead of helping convert them to the INFJ's viewpoint.

These failed efforts make evident that something is getting lost in translation. Jung offers a clue as to what that "something" might be, saying,

> *To the extent that (INJs) do not understand themselves—because they very largely lack (Introverted) judgment—they are also powerless to understand why they are so constantly underestimated by the public... also their communications are without the personal warmth that alone carries the power of conviction. On the contrary, these types have very often a harsh, repelling manner, though of this they are quite unaware and did not intend it.*[51]

In referencing their "harsh, repelling manner," Jung appears to be calling attention to the problem of INFJs' over-reliance on Extraverted Judging to do the heavy lifting where communicating the value of Ni insights is concerned. As we discussed in Chapter 3 on relationships, often, in INFJs' zeal to see others reap the rewards of their intuitive insights, the tone and tenor of communication rises to a level so shrill that others are instinctively driven to pull away.

The reason for this response–not always apparent to INFJs, mind you–is that when the volume reaches the sort of fever pitch described here, the medium is increasingly at odds with the message. Bluntly, it strikes others as fundamentally contradictory that they should heed the sort of insight from INFJs meant to bring the deep inner peace that comes from a place of higher spiritual awareness as long as INFJs fail to exude anything of that inner peace themselves. When confronted with this reality, many INFJs will stubbornly insist–not wrongly, I might add–that the insight and advice intended for others is no less true just because they haven't found a way to integrate it into their own lives personally; but that misses the point. What INFJs posing this argument have mistakenly assumed is that what others seek is *knowledge*–or insight–above authenticity.

I believe this is what Jung is referring to when he recounts "the personal warmth" that is often lacking in INFJs' communications with others. The problem is, while it's usually obvious to INFJs that they've been put here for the purpose of using their intuitive insight to help save others' souls, it is considerably less obvious that they have also been called upon to use that same insight to save their *own*. In truth: **the pearl serves the oyster as much or more than the man who discovers it.**

For the unconvinced, consider what a pearl actually is, at core: evidence of the oyster's own personal struggle with the grit of unwanted, however necessary, experience. This is an altogether different product from the unrefined nacre of intuitive knowledge lining the oyster's shell as a mere fact of its existence and whose value in its present form, as Jung notes, is too subjective to be rightly considered "wisdom" by the masses.

As it is, wisdom–*true* wisdom–which bears authenticity's hallmark, is only found at the *intersection* of knowledge and experience. But neither knowledge nor experience on its own can ever capture the transcendent entirety of what we as human beings universally recognize as "wisdom." For their part, INFJs have been asked to transform grains of inspiration into genuine pearls of wisdom–a feat that is only accomplished by reflexively adding something of themselves in the way of personal experience to the creation process. In other words, whatever potential value exists in the raw nacre of Introverted Intuition is practically worthless to all but the INFJ, who, *by design*, is meant to discover its utility for him or herself and apply it; only then does something resembling true and authentic wisdom begin to take shape.

Unfortunately, INFJs who have been misled into believing that their intuitive knowledge is meant for the exclusive benefit of others will never successfully manufacture a pearl. Rather, they will expend precious time and energy grifting and hustling to sell others on the value of mother of pearl as a suitable substitute for the real deal. While many INFJs can and do find "good enough" life success utilizing this method, the effort required to keep it up becomes increasingly laborious and unsustainable as time goes on. INFJs going down this path are plagued with an impending sense of doom arising from the subconscious awareness that continuing to exploit their reserve of raw goods just to peddle them out to others is eventually going to leave them with nothing for themselves.

Frustratingly, although INFJs may intuitively sense that they are headed in the wrong direction, they often lack the self-awareness and inner agency required to know what, *specifically*, about their behavior needs to change and implement it. Instead, INFJs' frustration is usually projected onto others as the source of their woes, citing inaccurate accusations that people are being selfish and unappreciative of their Ni insights which results in INFJs' normally generous and affable temperament evaporating as stinginess and resentment set in. Problematically, this shift in demeanor has the result of working against them even further as their unrefined intuitive offerings are now being served up with a side of angst that others (not surprisingly) find unappealing.

Eventually, as INFJs run out of takers, they begin to doubt the worth of what they're peddling, which in turn makes it harder to generate the enthusiasm required to successfully manufacture a sale, compounding their woes. According to Thompson, "This is generally the point at which the (INFJ's) tertiary function, Introverted Thinking.... steps in." She explains,

> *(The) tertiary function is helpful and enriching when our secondary function is well developed. It provides an outlet for "the other side" of our personality. For example, it prompts IN(F)Js to recognize that truth can be appropriated experientially as well as conceptually as a way of being, one that they feel in their senses and their bones.*[52]

Jung also alludes to the shift from a conceptual / outward focus to an experiential / inward focus that occurs once INFJs finally recognize the importance of their tertiary Ti, saying:

> *His (Introverted) judgment allows him to discern, though often only darkly, that he, as a man and a whole human being, is somehow involved in his vision, that it is not just an object to be perceived, but wants to participate in the life of the subject. Through this realization he feels bound to transform his* own *life.*[53]

In other words, INFJs who actually *live* their insights–who see their carefully crafted theories reflected back to them in their own life experience and then use that self-awareness to fine-tune their actions going forward are bequeathed a kind of calm, inner conviction that allows them to release the desperate need to convince others of the "rightness" of their intuitions as a result of having experienced Ni's value for themselves. Suddenly, as if by magic, INFJs who do the required inner work afforded by tertiary Ti find that their intuitive insights begin to sell themselves in a way that auxiliary Fe with its aggressive salesmanship never could on its own.

Perhaps it's because, having now done the inner work, INFJs are finally "relating to people," as Thomson says, instead of "counseling them or analyzing their frame of mind," that this notable shift in others' receptivity occurs. Afterall, the best teachers don't simply lecture, they *relate* to their students, learning with and from them, knowing intuitively when to advise and when to let them learn for themselves. Relatability requires a certain humility, or acceptance of one's flaws and imperfections, but this is only possible if INFJs have been subject to life's hardships to some degree, to the challenges of individuation and personal growth that arise in the context of relationships and other experiences that force INFJs to test their Ni mettle inwardly on themselves.

On closer inspection, it would appear that the universe has been attempting to nudge INFJs (sometimes not so gently) in this direction all along, toward developing greater inner agency instead of constantly relying on others' behavior (such as the acceptance of INFJs' insight and advice) to provide them with the peace they're seeking. Although the resistance that INFJs experience feels like a setback in the moment, like the well-known admonishment, "Physician heal thyself!", it's really an opportunity to examine what it is about *themselves* that requires further examination and revision. It's also an opportunity for INFJs to learn the art of self-soothing– an empowering skill that draws on a strong sense of inner agency–which is frequently lacking, not just in INFJs, but in Judgers generally.

The difficulty with getting Judging types to see the value in developing inner agency, however, is that their steadfast conviction that they can easily persuade others to bend to their will eliminates the need for them to modify their own behavior in their minds. (To be fair, experience bears this out: Judgers tend to be incredibly capable managers.) It's a belief that masks the reality that Judging types actually feel a corresponding lack of control over *themselves*, however subconscious. Stated alternately, Judgers instinctively seem to know what's in the best interest of others, but not always what's in their own. Being "frustrated" by the world provides

Judging types like INFJs an opportunity to go inward, to learn about themselves, and to find out how they can be empowered to manifest their own positive feelings, irrespective of others.

Unfortunately, as long as INFJs believe that the only way they can be happy is when outside circumstances–Fe, Se, or otherwise–align with their visions and desires, they will never find true inner peace since the possibility that circumstances might fail to conform to their expectations always exists. Afterall, as much as Judgers hate to admit it, some things are simply beyond our control. But INFJs who know that they can effectively change *themselves* even when they can't change the world around them–to "adapt," in other words–are bequeathed a complete psychospiritual arsenal, conferring a sense of peace in almost any circumstance. This is essentially what tertiary Ti development looks like for INFJs.

Truthfully, it is not an exaggeration to suggest that the realization of INFJs' inner strength, autonomy and agency represented by Ti might only be possible *because* INFJs have been pushed to a point of frustration with respect to their outer circumstances–a feat that is nigh impossible if INFJs always choose to play it safe. For what other reason would an oyster be compelled to transform nacre into pearl without some sort of irritant to motivate the action? Again, without the willingness on the part of INFJs to open themselves to experience, to face criticism or possibly even rejection from others–to risk discomfort over security to a large extent–there likely would be nothing incentivizing INFJs to develop Ti, and therefore no actualization.

• • •

There is nothing obviously beautiful or attention-grabbing about an oyster. Its rough variegations and dull brownish-gray tones lack the refined elegance of more outwardly showy mollusks like the conch or nautilus whose fantastic patterns and opalescent hues have long been a boon to shell-hungry beachcombers everywhere. But what seaside collector has ever stooped enthusiastically into the sand to retrieve an empty oyster shell? No self-respecting treasure hunter would—the shell itself having little to no apparent value. Rather, when it comes to the oyster, what every good shucker knows is, like the proverbial box of crackerjacks, the prize is *inside.* Still, just because every oyster can produce a pearl, doesn't mean that every oyster *does.*

INFJs are well aware of this fact. And many, if not all, live with the agonizing fear that their pearl-making potential will never amount to anything in actuality. Because they spend their early years as perceivers, largely waiting for life to happen *to* them (at least until they've gathered enough passive experience to permit some grit under the mantle, allowing them to produce something of value to give back to the world), much of their lives is seemingly spent in a state of latency. A considerable amount of time may pass—years, even—in which INFJs appear to accomplish very little of note or substance (just ask the family and friends who waited a small eternity for this book to be completed).

Indeed, to observe an oyster from the outside is to conclude that absolutely nothing is going on. But, consistent with their professed belief that much of what we observe about the world on its face belies its true inner nature, in order to be successful, INFJs must be prepared to let go of appearances and believe that something of worth *is* gestating inside of them even when the outside world has concluded that there isn't. That's because, as we've seen, putting too much weight on outer appearances and others' perceptions tends to entrap INFJs into taking on full-time jobs as rhetoricians and sermonizers, working Fe overtime to convince others of the merit of their unrefined insights rather than doing the transformational inner work afforded by Ti.

To undergo this transformation, INFJs have been given the necessary equipment in the form of a shell and flesh, along with a kind of unique primordial knowledge—what we call "potential"—to produce pearls. But, as essential as these factors are, they are merely a prerequisite for actualization, not an *ipso facto* guarantee. Excepting the externally sourced blessing deceptively disguised as a curse (aka the "grit"), a pearl is crafted with nothing but the diligence of self-determination, one painstaking layer at a time before eventually finding its way to an appreciating public for purposes that appear entirely selfish (it took every ounce of self-restraint not to use the word "shellfish"–but I digress.) This is the work of tertiary Ti: slow, steady, solitary and self-absorbed.

And yet, as Thomson astutely notes, "IN(F)Js don't find it easy to make this effort," since "developing secondary skills... forces compromises we don't want to make."[54] Arguably, the most difficult bridge in the function stack to cross is the one between the auxiliary and tertiary functions. Unlike the dominant and auxiliary functions which are more complementary in nature, the auxiliary and tertiary functions are diametrically opposed which makes shifting gears more of a challenge. For INFJs, there can be resistance to indulging in the perceived self-absorption of Ti which appears to be in direct contrast to Fe's "other-focused" nature. Doing so tends to come with the high price of guilt and anxiety as it risks disappointing others and incurring the hazards associated with neglecting the social safety net they've worked hard to build.

Ironically, it's often at the precise moment that INFJs are attempting to turn inward and focus on their Ti needs that others seem to demand their time and attention most, almost daring INFJs to stay away from Fe (that's how it feels from the INFJ's perspective, anyway.) But this phenomenon arguably occurs because INFJs have created the expectation of their ongoing involvement in other people's lives such that others are caught off-guard when they feel the INFJ pulling away for the first time. When this happens, the temptation to rush in and meet others' expectations can be so great that many INFJs never find a way to successfully breach the wall of resistance between Fe and Ti; but the fact remains that in order to go forward in development, INFJs are counterintuitively required to take what feels like a large step backward.

So what are INFJs to do when they find themselves pulled in two different directions, caught between opposing personality parts in the psyche? Thankfully (to put a Jungian twist on a well-known phrase in the current parlance), "There's a function for that!" What Jung fittingly dubbed "the transcendent function"–a psychological tool that aids us through the individuation process by helping the ego navigate and reconcile our conflicting functions–is, fortuitously enough, also a part of the personality equation. Jung elaborates:

> *If the mediatory product remains intact, it forms the raw material for a process not of dissolution but of construction, in which thesis and antithesis* (Fe and Ti in this case) *both play a part. In this way it becomes a new content that governs the whole attitude putting an end to the division and forcing the energy of the opposites into a common channel... I have called this process in its totality the* transcendent function... *(as) this function facilitates a transition from one attitude to another.*[55]

The beauty of the transcendent function is that, unlike the functions that comprise our primary function stack (Ni, Fe and so on...), it exists as a supraordinate process that overlays–or sits "atop"–the other functions. As Jung explains, the transcendent function is "the very stuff of the psyche, transcending time and dissolution; and its configuration by the opposites ensures its sovereign power over all the psychic functions."[56] Visualized as a gearshift, if our primary functions are symbolized by the various gears (drive, park, reverse, etc.), the transcendent function is the gearshift itself that enables us to move with relative ease between them.

And just as learning how to drive a stickshift is an art that requires both knowledge and experience to make the car go smoothly, so too is mastery of the transcendent function an essential skill for our psychological health and well-being. Yet, to suggest that the transcendent function is something that one effectively "masters" is rather misleading since, at least initially, the transcendent function cannot be brought about consciously, but instead tends to appear as a blessing from the unconscious in moments when ego consciousness has gotten stuck between two opposing functions. As Jung says, "the transcendent function is not something one does oneself; it comes rather from experiencing the conflict of opposites."[57]

With that said, the more encounters with the transcendent function we have over time, the easier it is to see it attempting to work in our lives, both practically and psychologically. When this happens, our job is to get out of our own way, ego wise, in order to make space for the transcendent function to enlighten us as to, what is sometimes referred to in spiritual circles as, "the third way." The "third way" reveals a path or option previously unknown to us that manages to satisfy the demands of *both* functions to the maximum extent possible–its chief aim being the edification of the Self. It does this by promoting into consciousness the most beneficial solution possible (aka "the greatest good") and, perhaps more importantly, allows us to accept with peace and grace whatever sacrifices must be endured to achieve it–even when the greatest good paradoxically appears to be in our own self-interest (as may be the case for INFJs struggling to set down others' Fe expectations to focus on their own Ti needs).

Spoto makes reference to the "third way", or what he calls "the middle realm," in his examination of the role of the transcendent function in psychological development:

> *This is hypothetically an area in which neither consciousness nor the unconscious has unfair advantage over the other. It exists in potentia as a field of opportunities for the personality to effect a temporary collaboration between two normally combative sides of the psyche.*[58]

It is from this place that real growth and personal development occurs: the tension and conflict of opposites being the fertile ground from which creativity–the source of spiritual and psychological life–eventually springs. In this way, the "ego" is effectively transcended and the larger Self emerges. Spoto continues:

> *The ego, realizing it is no longer at the center of the psyche, willingly acknowledges its attachment to something "other," to*

> *the Self about which it moves. This in effect allows consciousness itself more "mobility" to explore the psyche, to roam around the center rather than straining to keep the center for itself.*[59]

Simply put, the transcendent function provides a special brand of wisdom that ego consciousness on its own cannot; more accurately perhaps, the value of the transcendent function picks up where that of ego consciousness ends. And mercifully so, since without the intercession of the transcendent function we would find ourselves stuck in a state of perpetual cognitive dissonance without any hope of escape–a state that tends to give rise to a host of unfortunate psychological symptoms such as anxiety and depression, among other neuroses, which are directly correlated with a feeling of powerlessness. It has been my experience that finding oneself in this "stuck" state is a sure sign that we've lost touch with the wisdom of the transcendent function, inhibiting our ability to engage in what psychologist Susan David describes as "emotional agility" in her book of the same name.

Often, as David points out, we proceed according to an unconscious set of rules, values and habits adopted early in life for reasons we rarely, if ever, reconsider for present usefulness. The logic behind this is entirely rational: it expedites valuable processing time and conserves precious mental resources not to have to labor unnecessarily over every decision, large and small (of which there are literally hundreds, if not thousands, a day), allowing us to be more industrious over time. And yet this entirely rational behavior has a rather unfortunate side-effect in that it tends to promote psychological rigidity–a veritable death sentence for the Self. Afterall, anything that is not growing or evolving is effectively dead or dying.

On some level the unconscious knows this, and it beckons us to keep moving forward, to stay agile by seeking out new, life-giving alternatives found further down in the function stack–to *individuate,* in other words–despite the powerful ego forces working to keep us locked into familiar old patterns. The aim here is not to demonize the ego—for it has a clear place and purpose in the psychological complex—but rather to point out that the ego is meant to work *alongside* the unconscious for healthy development of the Self. To involuntarily be at the whim of ego impulses day in and out, however, is to relegate personal power and agency, rendering us more like performing monkeys rather than wise overseers with respect to our life's direction. But all of that changes when we decide to quit operating on autopilot by bringing conscious awareness to the unconscious process that is seeking expression inside of us.

To accomplish this, David argues, we must be prepared to "walk our why," which she describes as "the art of living by your own personal set of values—the beliefs and behaviors that you hold dear and that give you meaning and satisfaction." She continues:

> *Identifying and acting on the values that are truly your own—not those imposed on you by others; not what you think you should care about, but what you genuinely do care about—is the crucial next step of fostering emotional agility.*[60]

While I agree with her assessment, particularly as it pertains to values imposed on us by others, I would add the caveat that sometimes what we think we "genuinely" care about (i.e., what the ego cares about) misleads us into clinging to values that do not necessarily serve the Self and its plan for our larger development. In other words, it's not simply others' values that may be clouding or corrupting our personal values (and thus our emotional agility), but quite possibly our *own* values—at least as the ego identifies them—that are responsible for undermining our emotional agility to a large extent as well, creating that "stuck" state of cognitive dissonance referred to earlier.

There's a fairly simple work-around to this problem, however: by relocating our personal values from the narrow to the broad in scope—specifically, by prioritizing the development and advancement of the *Self* ahead of any one function and its associated values—we effectively open the door to emotional agility and, I would argue, to greater freedom, resilience, and happiness as a result. Sometimes, of course, the Self beckons us to adhere to the values of a specific function in a given moment (Fe may need to take priority when my husband urgently needs medical care requiring me to set aside my Ti work project for the day, for example). The fact is, our personal values shift depending on present circumstances, inner and outer, which are also in a constant state of flux; it's just so much easier to know "which of our values to value," so to speak, when we've got at least one eye on the transcendent function in addition to that which is always on the ego.

In truth, the Self never asks us to abandon the cornerstones of our identity altogether—values represented by the dominant and auxiliary functions. Those foundational values are an integral part of the unique equation that is our individual personality. However, the Self does seek to "round out" our dominant functions and fortify them through the incorporation of other parts of the personality that are still in need of development so that we may, in fact, become more emotionally, psychologically, and behaviorally agile. But whether or not we have the wisdom to listen and trust the Self when it reveals what needs further development frequently depends on us finding ourselves in a position where the ego is no longer able to maintain control of the steering wheel—these are the moments in which breakthroughs are born.

• • •

Arguably, the greatest gift that INFJs can give the world is that of their own personal growth. It's also the greatest gift they can give to *themselves*. That's because, when INFJs finally discover the inner strength and resilience that comes with investing in tertiary Ti, the Sensing world becomes a much less frightening place, eliminating INFJs' need to try to control or change it. This concept is beautifully summarized in a saying commonly attributed to the poet Rumi, who, though I'm paraphrasing, conveyed this same idea more or less along these lines: "In my cleverness I set out to change the world. In my wisdom I discovered that what really needed changing was myself; in so doing, the world changed." Another overused but apropos saying goes, "*Be* the change you wish to see the in the world."

Through the development of tertiary Ti, INFJs discover a different way to channel their Ni intuitions–from a focus that is largely outcome-oriented to one that is more process-oriented–resulting in the manufacture of the most valuable product of all: themselves. INFJs find that the treasure they desire is not something obtained from without, but actually a byproduct of their own personal growth and development–what we call living "inside-out." In other words, the Se result that INFJs have been seeking all this time (the "pearl") is really just the happy coincidence of doing what comes naturally to them: living out their days unearthing and applying intuition's insight not just for others, but also for themselves, for a more authentic and satisfying life experience.

The above revelation is responsible for successfully reducing and even eliminating INFJs' need to know the outcome of their efforts in advance. Afterall, the more rewarding the process, the less consequential the outcome. The act of writing this book is a perfect example; at the time I started I had no idea what the end result was going to be. But, truthfully, I did not need to know. And on further reflection, I can honestly say that I would not have *wanted* to know, as doing so would have largely robbed me of the experience of being pleasantly surprised by what emerged with each passing day. By being open to the unexpected, I unwittingly experienced life through Se lenses, taking whatever came as it came with a sense curiosity and excitement instead of fear and anxiety, fulfilling a key objective of the INFJ's actualization process.

Nevertheless, it may well be that, despite their newfound growth and development, the world rejects INFJs for their brand of authentic living anyway. It's entirely possible that others will find their pearls of wisdom worthless or, worse, threatening or objectionable in some way. The risks associated with these unfavorable outcomes are often enough for less developed INFJs to demur in the face of fear: *better to avoid the business of manufacturing pearls altogether*, the logic may go. But to be living–to be alive at this *very* moment, in other words–is to agree to an implicit contract with the universe to live in faith to a large degree and accept an untold number of unknowns with respect to the future. We are simply not promised specific outcomes. What we *are* promised, however, are certain gifts and tools unique to our personality to help us navigate, and even thrive, in the face of these unknowns. So, in spite of the risks, we are called to put ourselves out there–pardon the pun–"nacred and afraid" all the same.

INFJs with well-developed Ti understand this reality. Moreover, they don't feel personally victimized by their situation, but rather accept with a kind of graceful stoicism the fact that they have a job to do, if "only" for their own personal happiness, which makes it easier to go on with the business of Ni in their day-to-day lives, even when the outcome isn't guaranteed. Thomson backs up this observation, saying,

> *Such types... realize that some Intuitions will not bear fruit in a particular time and place. Sometimes the only responsible decision is to keep them alive and pass them down to the next generation. This is a hard notion in culture that values the gratifications of the present moment, but IN(F)Js often make a difference whose consequences they will never see.*[61]

On first read that last sentence may seem like something of a sad concession–the tragic refrain of INFJs not heard round the world. It seems sad, that is, until we realize that self-actualized INFJs have long since given up any concern about what happens to the pearl, having already crafted it for their selfsame benefit. In other words, because intuition has served its purpose for the INFJ–because it has already made a vast improvement in her own quality of life–whatever its consequences to the outside world are, frankly, incidental. Such nonchalance would be unthinkable to INFJs who have largely elided Ti in favor of Fe and Se. But the self-reflexive nature of Ti is that it acts as a lovely tempering agent to the excessive focus on outcomes that tends to beguile INFJs who repeatedly find themselves in the grip when events don't unfold the way they had planned.

There is profound peace and freedom for INFJs in being able to let go of responsibility for outer consequences–the kind that can only come from knowing that we've personally done all that we can do in a situation to influence a desirable outcome. Of course, that's incredibly difficult if we're not sure what it is that we're actually capable of. Such is the value of developing the entire function stack, especially tertiary Ti: it shows INFJs what it is they're capable of on an experiential level, and it allows them to let go of pretty much everything else.

Such experience also teaches INFJs that their personal happiness has always relied on using their Ni gifts to discern underlying truths, regardless of the outcome and whether or not it makes a difference in the lives of others (though it very often does.) Taking charge of our personal growth, development, and actualization, doing whatever we can to understand ourselves better and respond to the call before us–this is ultimately what authentic living looks like. And it's this quality of authentic living, and quite possibly only this quality, that can well and truly be called "beyond rare."

. GLOSSARY .

Collective Unconscious

According to Jung, involves "all psychic contents that belong not to one individual but to many, i.e., to a society, a people, or mankind in general." Hence, there's a sense in which humans seem to "know" things, or adopt certain roles (e.g., archetypes), without direct prior exposure or conscious learning.

Differentiation

The emergence of salient and identifiable parts or processes (e.g., functions) within the psyche. The more distinct or developed the part, the more it can be said to be differentiated.

Ego

The locus of our conscious personality and personal identity. While useful and necessary for navigating modern life, an unchecked ego can inspire personal, moral, and relational dysfunction; often contrasted with the Self (see below).

Ego Defensiveness

Heightened sensitivity or touchiness to perceived ego threats (e.g., "taking everything personally"). Commonly linked to the inferior function, which can be more vulnerable and sensitive to perceived slights.

Extraversion (Jungian)

Habitually directing one's energy and attention to outwardly, whether via Se, Ne, Te or Fe.

Extraverted Feeling (Fe)

The dominant function for EFJ types and auxiliary for INFJs. Emotionally connects with others; highly communicative, offers guidance and feedback; facilitates morale and consensus.

Extraverted Intuition (Ne)

The dominant function for ENP types. Broadly explores and envisions ideas, connections and possibilities; open, curious and creative.

Extraverted Judging

Collectively refers to Fe and Te, both of which are Extraverted and Judging functions.

Extraverted Perceiving

Collectively refers to Se and Ne, both of which are Extraverted and Perceiving functions.

Extraverted Sensing (Se)

The dominant function for ESP types and inferior for INFJs. "Lives in the moment"; relishes new experiences and challenges; attunes to concrete affairs and opportunities for action.

Extraverted Thinking (Te)

The dominant function for ETJ types. Rationally structures ideas, things and processes; consults established methods and data in research and decision-making.

Function

Defined by Jung as a "particular form of psychic activity that remains the same in principle under varying conditions." The eight functions in Jung's schema are: Ni, Si, Ne, Se, Fe, Te, Fi, and Ti.

Function Stack

Each personality type utilizes four (non-shadow) functions–dominant, auxiliary, tertiary, and inferior–prioritized according to their degree of proficiency and accessibility in consciousness. We refer to this functional hierarchy as the "function stack."

"Grip" Experiences

The sense of being locked into a single activity or mode of functioning. May initially resemble "flow experiences," in which we feel focused and engaged. In healthy flow experiences, however, psychological suppleness, receptiveness, and flexibility are retained. By contrast, grip experiences are marked by tunnel vision, loss of one's sense of humor, and an inability to shift gears. Often tied up in the inferior function, they can be addictive–begetting obsessive, compulsive, or otherwise dysfunctional behavior.

Individuation

Jung's term for the lifelong process of personal development and realizing one's potential as a particular personality type and individual.

Introversion (Jungian)

Habitually directing one's energy and attention inwardly, whether via Si, Ni, Ti, or Fi.

Introverted Feeling (Fi)

Dominant function for IFP types. Reflects on personal feelings and values; champions authenticity and individuality; drawn to nature, children and animals.

Introverted Intuition (Ni)

Dominant function for INJ types. Generates convergent insights and impressions; perspicacious; penetrates to discern foundational causes and patterns.

Introverted Judging

Collectively refers to Fi and Ti, both of which are Introverted and Judging functions.

Introverted Perceiving

Collectively refers to Si and Ni, both of which are Introverted and Perceiving functions.

Introverted Sensing (Si)

The dominant function for ISJ types. Stabilizes beliefs, decisions and behavior by drawing on past experience and instruction; embraces the "tried and true."

Introverted Thinking (Ti)

The dominant function for ITP types and tertiary for INFJs. Checks everything against inner logical standard; prefers autonomy in projects, problem-solving and decision-making.

Judging

According to type theory, Thinking and Feeling are "Judging" functions, used to impose order, make decisions and draw conclusions, either inwardly or outwardly. Myers-Briggs Judging (J) types habitually Extravert (i.e., outwardly express) Judging by way of Te or Fe.

Perceiving

Sensing and Intuition are considered "Perceiving" functions, used to acquire information, either inwardly or outwardly. Myers-Briggs Perceiving (P) types habitually Extravert Perceiving by way of Se or Ne.

Psychic

Pertaining to the *psyche*, which Jung viewed as the totality of all conscious and unconscious psychological processes.

Self

The Self (capital "S") is the totality of our conscious and unconscious personality traits, or what Jung called the "unity of the personality as a whole." Since the perspectives of the Self (aka, the "greater or higher Self") are less narrow and short-sighted than those of ego consciousness, the Self is often considered psychospiritually "wiser."

Sensing / Sensation

One of Jung's four basic functions which he defined as the "function that mediates the perception of physical stimulus." He added that Sensation is primarily "sense perception–mediated by the sense organs and body senses (kinesthetic, vasomotor sensation, etc.)." He also associates it with *aesthetic* perception, which he considered more abstract than ordinary sense perception.

Shadow

According to Jung, "The shadow coincides with the 'personal' unconscious... (and) personifies everything that the subject refuses to acknowledge about himself... for instance, inferior traits of character and other incompatible tendencies." It also includes the shadow functions (i.e., 5th-8th), believed to be almost entirely unconscious.

Transcendent Function

The word *transcendent* indicates something which is "beyond" or "above." The transcendent function can thus be envisioned as "hovering above" the other functions. Its general purpose is to furnish wisdom and awareness, including discerning when it's contextually appropriate to use (or not use) a given function.

. SOURCES .

1. Jung, CG. *CW XI*, Para 144.

2. Jung, CG. *CW XVII*, Para 289.

3. Williams, T. *The Glass Menagerie.* 1944.

4. Einstein, A. *Letter to Dr. H. L. Gordon.* May 3, 1949.

5. Thomson, L. *Personality Type.* 1998. p. 246.

6. Ibid.

7. Keirsey, D. *Please Understand Me II.* 1998. p. 153.

8. Thomson, L. *Personality Type.* 1998. p. 230.

9. Ibid, pp. 343-344.

10. Ibid, p. 345.

11. Ibid, pp. 231, 234.

12. Laney, MO. *The Introvert Advantage.* 2002. pp. 252-253.

13. Thomson, L. *Personality Type.* 1998 p. 235.

14. Ibid, pp. 229, 231.

15. Wikipedia. "Analysis Paralysis." 2021.

16. Spoto, A. *Jung's Typology in Perspective.* 1995. p. 92.

17. Von Franz, ML. *Lectures on Jung's Typology.* 1984. pp. 6-7.

16. Spoto, A. *Jung's Typology in Perspective.* 1995. p. 89.

19. Ibid, p. 88.

20. Ibid, p. 77.

21. Ibid, pp. 91-92.

22. Ibid, p. 92.

23. Von Franz, ML. *Lectures on Jung's Typology.* 1984. pp. 6-7.

24. Spoto, A. *Jung's Typology in Perspective.* 1995. p. 91.

25. Von Franz, ML. *Lectures on Jung's Typology.* 1984. p. 66.

26. Jung, CG. *The Archetypes and Collective Unconscious.* 1969. pp. 285-285.

27. Jung, CG. *CW 9ii,* Para. 13-15.

28. Jung, CG. *CW 11,* Para. 134.

29. Ibid, Para. 292.

30. Ibid.

31. Quenk, NL. *Beside Ourselves.* 1993. p. 199.

32. Spoto, A. *Jung's Typology in Perspective.* 1995. p. 100.

33. Jung, CG. Zarathustra Seminar. pp. 1391-1392.

34. Jung, CG. *Psychological Types.* 1971. p. 401.

35. Von Franz, ML. *Lectures on Jung's Typology.* 1984. p. 15.

36. Ibid, p. 13.

37. Ibid, pp. 9, 11.

38. Ibid, p. 17.

39. Spoto, A. *Jung's Typology in Perspective.* 1995. p. 94.

40. Quenk, NL. *Beside Ourselves.* 1993. p. 57.

41. Thomson, L. *Personality Type.* 1998. p. 233.

42. Jung, CG. *Psychological Types.* 1971. p. 401.

43. Spoto, A. *Jung's Typology in Perspective.* 1995. pp. 102-103.

44. Jung, CG. *CW XI,* Para 391.

45. Jung. *Psychology and Alchemy*. 1980. p. 99.

46. Jung, CG. *Memories, Dreams, Reflections*. 1961.

47. Jung, CG. *Psychological Types*. 1971. p. 404.

48. Jung, CG. *Psychological Types*. 1971. p. 401.

49. Ibid.

50. Thomson, L. *Personality Type*. 1998. p. 237.

51. Jung, CG. *Psychological Types*. 1971. p. 403.

52. Thomson, L. *Personality Type*. 1998. p. 237.

53. Jung, CG. *Psychological Types*. 1971. p. 402.

54. Thomson, L. *Personality Type*. 1998. p. 238.

55. Jung, CG. *Psychological Types*. 1971. p. 480.

56. Ibid.

57. Jung, CG. *Letters Vol. 1*, p. 269.

58. Spoto, A. *Jung's Typology in Perspective*. 1995. p. 132.

59. Ibid, pp. 132-33.

60. David, S. *Emotional Agility*. 2016. p. 115.

61. Thomson, L. *Personality Type*. 1998. p. 239.

. BIBLIOGRAPHY .

Aron, E. *The Highly Sensitive Person.* Harmony. 1997.

David, S. *Emotional Agility: Get Unstuck, Embrace Change, and Thrive in Work and Life.* Penguin Random House. 2016.

Drenth, AJ. *The 16 Personality Types: Profiles, Theory and Type Development.* Inquire Books. 2013.

Drenth, AJ. *My True Type: Clarifying Your Personality Type, Preferences and Functions.* Inquire Books. 2014.

Jung, CG. *Memories, Dreams, Reflections.* Vintage. 1961.

Jung, CG. *Psychology and Alchemy.* Princeton University Press. 1980.

Jung, CG. *Psychological Types.* Princeton University Press. 1971.

Jung, CG. *The Archetypes and Collective Unconscious.* Princeton University Press. 1969.

Keirsey, D. *Please Understand Me II.* Prometheus Nemesis. 1998.

Laney, MO. *The Introvert Advantage: How Quiet People Can Thrive in an Extrovert World.* Workman Publishing. 2002.

Quenk, NL. *Beside Ourselves: Our Hidden Personality in Everyday Life.* Consulting Psychologists Press. 1993.

Spoto, A. *Jung's Typology in Perspective.* Chiron Publications. 1995.

Thomson, L. *Personality Type: An Owner's Manual.* Shambhala. 1998.

Von Franz, ML. *Jung's Typology.* BookCrafters. 1984.

. INDEX .

Learn

MORE

To learn more about INFJs, the other personality types, the functions, type theory and more, or to read Elaine's bio, visit:

PersonalityJunkie.com

Made in United States
North Haven, CT
19 August 2024

56215710R00114